T0064878

ENGLAND IN THE AGE OF CHIVALRY

. . . And Awful Diseases

ENGLAND IN THE AGE OF CHIVALRY

. . . And Awful Diseases

The Hundred Years' War and Black Death

ED WEST

Skyhorse Publishing

Skyhorse Publishing books may be purchased in bulk at special discounts for sales promotion, corporate gifts, fund-raising, or educational purposes. Special editions can also be created to specifications. For details, contact the Special Sales Department, Skyhorse Publishing, 307 West 36th Street, 11th Floor, New York, NY 10018 or info@skyhorsepublishing.com.

Skyhorse® and Skyhorse Publishing® are registered trademarks of Skyhorse Publishing, Inc.®, a Delaware corporation.

Visit our website at www.skyhorsepublishing.com.

10 9 8 7 6 5 4 3 2 1

Library of Congress Cataloging-in-Publication Data is available on file.

Cover design by Rain Saukas

Print ISBN: 978-1-5107-1988-0
Ebook ISBN: 978-1-5107-1993-4

Printed in the United States of America

Contents

Introduction

In February 1308, the king and queen of England were crowned at the newly finished St. Paul's Cathedral in London, a heavily ritualized coronation ceremony that dated back to the time of the Vikings and represented God's anointment of the monarch.

The new queen, Isabella, was the twelve-year-old daughter of France's King Philippe Le Bel, 'the handsome,' and had inherited her father's good looks. With thick blonde hair and large blue, unblinking eyes, she possessed great intelligence and cunning, cruelty as well as compassion, and a skill for hiding her feelings. Her new husband, King Edward II, was a brainless, boneheaded man of twenty-four years whose idea of entertainment was watching court fools fall off tables.

It was a fairy-tale coronation for the young girl. Well, apart from the fact that a plaster wall collapsed, bringing down the high altar and killing a member of the audience. And that the king was gay, and spent the afternoon fondling his lover Piers Gaveston while ignoring the queen.

Edward had put Gaveston, newly created as Earl of Cornwall, in charge of the ceremony, and the king and 'keeper of the realm' sat side by side beneath a coat of arms displayed on the wall, arms not of the new royal couple but the king and earl.[1] After the ceremony,

Edward went and sat with his 'minion' rather than the queen, and the two continued to touch each other throughout.

Gaveston also upstaged Isabella on her special day by wearing flamboyant clothes, according to one eyewitness 'so decked out that he more resembled the god Mars than an ordinary mortal.' The royal favorite was dressed in imperial purple embroidered with pearls, a provocatively regal outfit unsuitable for a courtier from a minor noble family, probably done deliberately to annoy the queen and her relatives. Most insulting of all, Gaveston was wearing the jewels that Isabella's father had given to Edward as his wedding present; the French king's other gifts, including prize warhorses, had also been handed over to his lover. A London chronicler said 'rumors circulated that the king was more in love with this artful and malevolent man than his bride, that truly elegant lady, who is a most beautiful woman.'

And to cap it all off, Gaveston was put in charge of the catering and managed to ruin it all with undercooked chicken. Understandably, the new queen was rather upset by the day's events, while her uncles, Louis and Charles, stormed out of the coronation banquet and returned to France, after 'seeing that the king frequented Piers's couch more than the queen's.'[2] (Visiting England, they must have been prepared for the worst on the culinary front.)

Gaveston also managed to hugely irritate the country's leading barons that day. The Coronation is a heavily symbolic and ancient event that day. dates back to King Edgar in 973, and like the Frankish ceremonies it was based on, it represented divine approval. But for everyone who was anyone, it was also a big party in which they got to show how important they were. Instead, Gaveston was given roles that were traditionally carried out by the great noble families who, it must be remembered, also had their own private armies. He got to carry the crown, as well as the *curtana*, 'the sword of mercy,' which was placed on the altar until redeemed by the king with an offer of gold; and he got to do the fixing of a spur to the king's left foot. That Gaveston landed these roles angered the leading barons so much it began a feud so bitter that after twenty years most of the leading players had been brutally murdered.

Edward and Isabella's marriage, rather unsurprisingly, did not end well; but the uniting of the English and French royal families that resulted from their wedding was a far bigger disaster. King Philippe died in 1314, months after burning to death the leaders of the chivalric order the Knights Templar, whose Grand Master had shouted from the flames a curse on Philippe and his house. His three sons would all die young, none of them leaving male descendants. Only one of Philippe's grandsons would survive to become a king, Isabella's son Edward—and his claim to the French throne would then plunge the two countries into a bitter, horrific conflict that in the Victorian age became known as the Hundred Years' War.

Over the next few decades, France would be devastated by enormous bands of desperados, criminals, and bloodthirsty mercenaries plundering the countryside, to such an extent that large numbers of people took to living in caves. Whole towns were destroyed and their populations murdered. It was the worst war of the European medieval period, but it also marked its end, as the dominance of aristocratic knights was destroyed first by the longbow, and later by firearms.

Historians call this period 'the crisis of the Late Middle Ages' and one reason it appears so grim is that for so long people had finally been having it good—well, relatively. After centuries of chaos and misery traditionally called the 'Dark Ages,' western civilization had in the twelfth century exploded: the first universities were founded, literacy vastly increased, Europe produced great philosophers for the first time in centuries, cathedrals were built, stone houses replaced wood, internal warfare declined, and in most areas of technology Christians equaled the ancients. The 'feudal anarchy' of the eleventh century, a war of everyone against everyone, evolved into increasingly stable and organized central authorities, with Church-sanctioned peace creating the conditions for trade, industry, and art.

The population swelled, as did levels of trade with the continent. Cities like London for the first time reached their Roman-era numbers. A rising population meant a bigger pool of labor and more hungry mouths, before agricultural technology had allowed Europe to escape the Malthusian trap, which is the theory first pointed out by Rev. Thomas Malthus that population growth exceeds food production and so leads to famine. (Agricultural improvements in the past two hundred years have so far disproved this, but until then it was not possible.) The real wage rates of English farm workers, which can be calculated from the early thirteenth century onward, had plunged to their lowest yet. Immense pressure was placed on resources and diet; people were a lot smaller than two centuries earlier, with many suffering from bone diseases and weakened immune systems.

The mild weather of this era, an unusually hot few centuries called the Medieval Warm period, had allowed Europe to produce more food—but now the earth cooled and, as a result, in 1315, the spring after the Templars were burned in Paris, the continent was hit by severe rains and the crops failed. The Great Famine of 1315–1317 killed as many as one in ten people in England, but even this was not the worst thing that happened that century. That dubious honor went instead to the Black Death, the rat-borne disease of the 1340s that ended the lives of between a third and a half of Europe. The population of England, five million in 1300, had fallen to just half that a century later.[3]

Even to those not coughing out plague-ridden black blood, life was unimaginably grim—half of people died before twenty, and life expectancy could be as low as eighteen in some poorer parts of England.[4] Although infancy was the most dangerous time, even those who reached adulthood and lived a relatively long life would have endured various chronic illnesses and pains. Not that 'childhood' in the modern sense really existed; medieval boys worked from age seven and could be hanged at that age. Girls could expect to be pregnant by fourteen, a condition they would endure for much of the next two decades, at a time when one in sixty labors ended in the mother's death. By the time they were thirty they were worn out or, as Geoffrey Chaucer put it, 'winter forage.'

And plague, famine, and war weren't even the only disasters. There was also a split in the Catholic Church between two men claiming to be pope, one a ruthless mass murderer and the other clearly insane, causing much suffering and death. In the middle of the century there was a disastrous banking collapse in Italy, as well as a number of large earthquakes. France and England both saw extremely violent rural uprisings. Everything that could go wrong went wrong, and many writers lamented that the world was coming to an end.

Yet this period also gave us some of the greatest works of art and poetry, by the likes of Giotto, Dante, Boccaccio and, in England, Geoffrey Chaucer. Painting was transformed in this period, so that the king who ended the century, Richard II, is presented in full renaissance glory in the *Wychton Tripdich*, one of England's most famous artworks. The period also saw the most important development in constitutional history, the birth of the House of Commons, and the establishment of Parliament as the lawmaking body on which the monarch depended. It all began with Edward II's terrifying father and his insatiable appetite for war.

CHAPTER ONE

Long Live the King

Edward II had not had the easiest childhood, being the young-est of sixteen children to Eleanor of Castile and the violent maniac Edward Longshanks, confusingly called Edward I even though he was the fourth king of England to be named that.[1]

The first Edward, standing at six foot three, was a domineering, terrifying figure also nicknamed 'the Hammer of the Scots' as well as 'the Leopard,' after a then-common belief that the animal could change its spots, as he had a habit of going back on his word. He was also known as 'the Lawgiver' or 'the English Justinian,' after the Roman emperor, as he introduced laws firmly establishing Parlia-ment, and in particular created the House of Commons, although without really meaning to.[2]

Edward had become king in 1272 after the long reign of his sim-pleminded father Henry III. Longshanks's grandfather King John had been such a disaster that, after alienating everyone through his lechery, drunken violence, and cowardice, his barons had forced on him a peace treaty that later became known as Magna Carta, which he immediately ignored.[3] Following a year of subsequent civil war, John died of dysentery in late 1216, having gorged himself to death on food and alcohol, and left his nine-year-old son in charge, so broke he could not even afford a crown for his coronation and with his enemies in control of the majority of the country. But, thanks to the heroic elderly knight William Marshal who led the loyalist forces into battle despite being in his seventies, young Henry survived to become one of the longest reigning monarchs in English history.

The essential cause of the conflict had been how much the barons could restrain the king, and who paid for what, and after the First Barons' War of 1215–17 the same problems arose again in the 1250s. The rebel leader this time was a mildly psychotic French knight called Simon de Montfort who led on a platform of low-self-awareness populist xenophobia despite living a fantastically luxurious lifestyle and having only arrived in England in his twenties without speaking a word of English. He was also married to King Henry's sister, and the king was terrified of him.

Henry's eldest son Edward had grown up during this difficult period. Apart from sharing a lazy eye, father and son were nothing alike. Henry was an absentminded simpleton who managed to get lost in the one battle he took part in; his eldest son, named after the eleventh-century saint Edward the Confessor, was a bloodthirsty maniac whose lifelong ambition was to go on a Crusade and bring Jerusalem back to Christianity in an orgy of violence.

Like most young aristocrats, Edward was trained for war through 'tourneys,' or jousts, which had begun in western France in the eleventh century as sort of toleration zones for violence. Although we have in our minds an idea of tournaments as colorful events where men got to show off to women waving handkerchiefs, they were incredibly violent affairs that often ended in multiple fatalities; in 1240 during a tourney outside Dusseldorf, sixty knights were killed in one event. But neither this nor Church condemnation made the slightest bit of difference to the endless supply of aristocratic yobs who loved these events. In June 1256, around the time of his seventeenth birthday, Edward took part in his first tourney at Blyth in Nottinghamshire, at which a number of jousters died from their wounds.

During the early stages of de Montfort's protests, Edward had sided with his uncle, but as it became more violent he returned to his father, and it was Edward who won the war at the battle of Evesham in 1265. It didn't end well for de Montfort: before the battle, Edward assembled a hit squad of a dozen men, the 'strongest and most intrepid at arms' to kill his uncle, who ended up being chopped into a number of parts, and his testicles hung around his nose. (Edward's ally Roger Mortimer struck the killer blow and so his wife got to keep de Montfort's head.)

Many considered Edward's behavior after the battle, when he executed a number of de Montfort supporters, to be murder, but this ruthlessness was characteristic. As a young man, he once ordered his attendants to put out the eyes and crop the ears of an adolescent who angered him. The gossipy monk Matthew Paris tells a story about Longshanks being out with his followers one day when he gratuitously orders the mutilation of one man, just for larks. Such was his reputation that the Archbishop of York had an interview with the king, and afterwards was so shaken he took to his bed and simply died. Another cleric, sent by his fellow priests to complain to the king about taxation, fell down dead on the spot.

Then there was an incident in 1303, when Edward's treasury was burgled and crown jewels stolen; after the culprits were caught, he had the thieves' skin nailed to the treasury door. The royal account book of 1297 includes the cost of repairing his daughter Elizabeth's coronet, which Edward had thrown into the fire in a rage. And, like any great psychotic medieval despot, he was an enthusiastic persecutor of Jews.

Still, Edward was very loving to his pet falcon, and he even used to visit the shrine of Thomas Beckett to offer prayers for his bird, and made a wax image of the sick animal—so not entirely a bad person.

Before becoming king of England, he had been put in charge of Gascony, the region of southwest France still ruled by the English monarch. On one occasion, Edward was dealing with Gascon rebels who had holed up in a church in La Reole, and ordered it destroyed only for his father to overrule him (Henry loved churches). Gascony formed part of the Duchy of Aquitaine, which had become part of the English crown after the ill-fated marriage of Henry II and its heiress Eleanor of Aquitaine in 1152 (it wasn't very happy—he imprisoned her for fifteen years). After their son John had lost most of his French territory in 1204, Gascony remained the last part of the continent attached to the English crown, but the French claimed it. Still, it does produce very good wine so we can see their point, and at the time, Gascony sold five million gallons of the stuff to England every year—some twenty-five million bottles, a large amount when it was very expensive to import.

With England at peace, beginning in1269 Edward took up the gap year of his day, the Crusades. He wanted to do what every young rich kid did: take a year off, experience new cultures, see some really interesting countries, kill all the inhabitants, then go home and bore everyone senseless talking about it. Strangely enough, he brought his wife Eleanor of Castile with him, even though they already had two kids.

The couple had been married since 1254, when they were both children, and were devoted to each other. While on Crusade, Eleanor gave her husband *Concerning Matters Military*,[4] or *De Re Militari*, a book on war by the late Roman writer Vegetius. It was sort of the *How to Win Friends and Influence People* of its time and read by everyone who mattered. The couple had an enduring romantic attachment unusual for the age, and unlike most medieval kings, Edward had no mistresses.[5]

The plan had been to go on joint Crusade with his cousin, King Louis of France. However, the whole adventure was ruined when, after decades of planning, the French at the last minute chose to head to North Africa instead, where Louis soon died (later becoming Saint Louis on rather dubious grounds). Edward ended up first in Tunis and later in Palestine where he fought Sultan Baibars, a Turkish leader who occasionally skinned prisoners alive, according to one chronicler.

However, by the time Edward arrived in the Holy Land, the Crusades were as good as lost and, in 1272, he made preparations to return home; before he left, though, he was almost killed in Haifa, in modern-day Israel, at the hands of the Assassins, an Islamic cult led by an enigmatic figure called 'the old man in the mountain' who trained young fanatics to become suicide-killers. An assassin, after securing a private audience with Edward, took out his dagger and stabbed him before Edward overpowered and killed the man; however, the knife was poisoned, and Edward's life was only saved when his wife sucked out the poison. This part of the story sounds slightly unlikely, but its popularity reflected the genuine love match that existed between the two.[6]

This was just one of many amazing scrapes the adventurous king survived, on top of storms at sea, two battles in which he came out unscathed, and a miraculous escape after his horse slipped at Winchelsea, which should have crushed him. Edward was once playing chess and then got up to stretch his legs for no reason, 'only to have a stone crash down from the vaulting in the place where he had been seated,' crushing his chair 'to matchwood.'[7] After this, he became devoted to the shrine of Our Lady at Walsingham in Norfolk, the holiest place in England, convinced that someone up there was looking out for him.

Edward was nowhere near as religious as his father, or credulous; he could easily spot frauds, of which there were many at the time, such as a knight who claimed to have had his blindness cured at the tomb of Henry III and whom the king dismissed as a liar. Henry had devoted years and vast amounts of money to rebuilding Westminster Abbey, originally constructed by his hero Edward the Confessor, but at the end of Longshank's thirty-five-year reign almost no work had been done at the still-unfinished church. He did own a huge number of relics, including a nail from the Cross and a saint's tooth 'effective against lightning and thunder,' but these could be seen more as valuables than any great display of faith.

In 1272, Edward was in Sicily when news reached him that his father had died, and also came news of the death of his son, John, aged just five. When the Sicilian king John of Anjou marveled that he mourned just the former, Edward said he could make another son but fathers were irreplaceable. Edward and Eleanor had sixteen children in total, of whom only four outlived him. The king was a very unsympathetic figure, but life was extremely grim for everyone and there was no room for sentiment.

It was another two years before the king arrived home, like any gap-year kid having come back with huge debts,[8] and on his way back he was invited to a tournament with one thousand English knights in Chalon-sur-Saone in Burgundy. The event turned out to be so violent that the pope himself condemned it, with many of the French *chevaliers* clearly trying to kill the king. He never fought in a tourney after that.

It seems strange for any young man to not even bother to return for his father's funeral, especially when he had inherited the crown of England, but having personally removed the testicles of the last man who had caused trouble, he correctly doubted that anyone else would try their luck. Because the new monarch was so far away, the king's council started a tradition by declaring that the new reign had begun immediately, rather than how previous reigns began when the crown jewels and armory were seized and any rivals thrown out of the nearest window. It is for this reason that the phrase 'the king is dead, long live the king' was invented, and why a half-mast flag was not flown at Buckingham Palace when a royal died again until 1997, when the tradition was changed after the death of Princess Diana.

After the crown was put on Edward's head, he theatrically took it off and said 'he would never take it up again until he had recovered the lands given away by his father to the earls, barons, and knights of England, and to aliens.' This wasn't going to end well.

CHAPTER TWO

The Round Table

Edward's coronation was a lavish affair and the feasting lasted two weeks. One hundred Scottish knights who turned up allowed their horses to run free and declared that anyone who caught one could keep it, and because of this act of reckless generosity the English knights felt the need to do the same. Two years earlier England had experienced famine, the first of many over the next half century, but such lavish flaunting of wealth was common because the entire medieval hierarchy was based on the idea that lords had to be able to entertain those below them. This is what caused kings and barons to ruin themselves and encouraged wars where they would get rich on plunder or die trying. The pinnacle of this idea of kingship was the mythical King Arthur, who, when not winning battles or showing his chivalrous qualities with the ladies, was looking after his improbably large entourage with great feasts and a constant supply of goodies. Arthur was Edward's role model and inspired his desire to become King of Britain, a dream that did much to form the identities of the island's three nations—England, Scotland, and Wales—although this was the opposite of what he intended.

The whole story of Arthur was basically made up by twelfth-century churchman Geoffrey of Monmouth who passed it off as history, and it became immensely popular across Western Europe. The Arthurian legend also fed into the evolving idea of chivalry, which as the medieval period went on became more like its modern ideal, celebrating knights who were brave and dashing but also compassionate and Christian.

The Arthur myth was based on the obscure wars of the Dark Ages between native Britons and invaders from the continent, the Angles and Saxons, who referred to their enemies as 'foreigners,' or *Welsh*; although by Edward's time they had come to refer to themselves as *Cymru*, 'the people' (today the Welsh nationalist party is called Plaid Cymru). Relations between the Welsh and English had never been warm, although the border had been stabilized in the eighth century by King Offa of Mercia, who built a dike to mark it.

Then, however, the Normans turned up, and after conquering England they created a series of semi-independent territories on the border, known as the Marcher Lordships ('march' means border, from where we get such words as marquis, Mercia, and Denmark). The Marcher lords tended to be the toughest and greediest of the Norman aristocrats, which is saying something, and were often in conflict with the monarch. They had also begun to encroach into Wales, grabbing the low-lying fertile land and settling it with English and Flemish migrants.[1] The Welsh, understandably, weren't entirely pleased, but because of its mountainous geography it was impossible to unite the country under one ruler. However, in the 1260s, a strong leader called Llywelyn ap Gruffydd became the first man to be recognized as Prince of Wales; then he refused to turn up to Edward's coronation in the confident belief he could snub him— hence his name, 'Llywelyn the Last.'

Llywelyn was a big fish in a small pond; he had a court large enough to include a bard, a harpist, falconers, and a 'silentiary,' whose job it was to keep the rowdiness to an acceptable level. But he was small-fry compared to Edward, and didn't even control all of Wales, which was divided among him and his three brothers, including Daffyd, who back in 1272 had plotted to assassinate his elder sibling. Forgiven by Llywelyn, he went on to conspire against him on a second occasion, this time with their brother Owain, before a snowstorm forced them to abort and run off to England where Daffyd was sheltered by the king.

As a result, the Welsh prince refused to attend the coronation. Edward demanded he pay his respects, and when Llywelyn again refused, the king of England even traveled up to Chester to save on the Welsh leader's travel expenses. Again, the prince declined, and in total Edward sent Llywelyn five summons, determined to have his way.

The Welshman sent three replies, explaining that he was waiting until their differences were sorted out, namely that Edward hand over the rebels. To add further insult, the fifty-something Llywelyn then married Eleanor, the twenty-three-year-old daughter of Simon de Montfort and Edward's aunt, Princess Eleanor, without the king's permission, and in fact without even having met her. (Strangely, it was possible at the time to marry someone without meeting them so long as an agreed substitute turned up at the wedding). It was this that set off Edward's slightly crazed mission to conquer all of Britain, using the Arthurian fantasy as his justification.

Wales was, for most Englishmen, still a wild and strange place, its people thought to be ruthless and bloodthirsty. In deepest Wales (*pura Wallia*), where the Normans had not settled and where Llywelyn's rule held sway, the old Laws of King Hywel Dda still applied; disputes were settled by blood feuds, and a thief would be pardoned if he had passed ten houses and 'failed to obtain anything to eat' before committing his crime. To the Normans, of course, starvation was no excuse for theft and would inevitably result in some important body part being removed.

In 1276, Edward raised an army and the following year invaded Wales, the English troops advancing under the flag of St. George they had brought back from Crusade; Llywelyn soon surrendered but was allowed to retain the title of Prince of Wales, partly as a sort of mockery to rub in how powerless he was. Edward had kidnapped his cousin Eleanor while she was en route to marry the Welsh leader, but now agreed to the match; however, she died in childbirth, and he had her daughter imprisoned almost from birth in case she might prove a rallying point for rebellion. She lived to her fifties, a captive her entire life, and an illustration of what a lovely man Edward was.

War broke out again in 1282, this time started by Daffyd, after which his elder brother felt obliged to join in an obviously doomed rebellion. The Archbishop of Canterbury tried to meditate, and an offer was made whereby Daffyd had to go on Crusade with Edward while Llywelyn would be given a big estate in England. The Welsh leader gave a romantic response by saying he would not betray his people; romantic, but obviously insane, as they didn't stand a chance. By the end of 1282, all Welsh resistance was over. Llywelyn died on December 11 at the hands of a common English soldier in Powys who had failed to recognize him as a valuable hostage.

Daffyd was soon captured and convicted of treason, murder, sacrilege, and plotting against the king, and his sentence was four corresponding punishments: respectively, dragged by horses, hanged, disemboweled, and quartered. Before he was dead, his intestines were slashed from his body and burned in front of him; his corpse was then sent to various English cities, and his head placed on a spike at the Tower of London, along with his brother's. At the English garrison at Shrewsbury, where Daffyd was killed, a fight broke out between the London and Yorkshire contingent over who got the head, which the Cockneys won. Not the most dignified end, all in all.

In 1284, Edward passed the Statute of Wales, formally ending its independence. To this day, Wales is technically part of England, which is why only England, Scotland, and Ireland are represented on the Union Jack.

There had long been a prophecy among the Britons that the 'lost lands' of England would be recovered and that a Welshman would again one day wear a crown in London. Llywelyn sort of fulfilled that, except it was as a rotting corpse, and the English had stuck a crown of ivy on his head in mockery. His decomposing head remained on a spike at the Tower of London for fifteen years before someone thought to take it down.

The new king cemented his control over Wales by building a series of castles, many of which still stand, among them Caernarfon, Flint, Rhuddlan, Conwy, Criccieth, and Aberystwyth. These could be defended with as few as twenty soldiers and, with stairs that led directly to the sea, withstand a siege for several years. Edward's castles in Wales were inspired by a knight from Savoy with the odd name of Othon de Grandson who had gone on Crusade with Edward and became his right-hand man from the mid-1260s, and these grand monuments were supposed to reflect his claim to be Arthur's heir as ruler of Britain. Edward chose Caernarfon as a site because it was believed that the father of the brutal fourth-century Roman emperor Constantine the Great, one of Edward's heroes, was buried there. (Constantine legalized Christianity but he also killed his own son and wife, along with countless others, so he was not absolutely guaranteed to get into heaven.) Caernarfon became a focus for Edward's megalomania. It was a small village in which he built an enormous castle based on the great city of Constantinople, complete with Roman-style imperial eagles. In fairness to Edward, though, the Welsh tourist industry does pretty well today thanks to his fantastic Arthurian castles.

While in Caernarfon, he claimed to have discovered the body of Emperor Magnus Maximus, who, according to Welsh legend, was the father of Constantine, even though he lived after him, and the grandfather of Arthur who lived three hundred years later. Maximus had supposedly dreamed of a maiden living in a castle and tracked her down and married her, her home supposedly being on the site of the future Caernarfon Castle.

The great Marcher lord, Roger Mortimer, who was Llywelyn's deadly enemy, held the first Arthurian Round Table event at Kenilworth Castle in Warwickshire in 1279. Mortimer's mother was Welsh and he claimed descent from the mythical king. The event featured one hundred knights and one hundred ladies, and at the end Mortimer was presented with barrels which everyone assumed contained wine but were actually full of gold. These Round Tables were sort of sanitized, family-friendly versions of tourneys in which women attended and there was far less bloodshed.

In 1284, Edward accepted the supposed Crown of Arthur—another dubious relic—for an even bigger Round Table feast in north Wales, along with the bones of Maximus. Although the mythical King Arthur, had he existed, would have surely supported the Welsh against the English, the legend increasingly became co-opted to justify the unification of Britain. Edward even had two corpses found a century earlier at Glastonbury Abbey under mysterious circumstances reinterred as 'Arthur and Guinevere.' It is recorded that Edward's Round Table party in north Wales was so popular, with attendees coming from all over the realm, that the floor gave way. Edward may have taken this as a sign of how loved he was, although since the last person who snubbed one of his invitations ended up having his head used as a football, it's hardly surprising that there were no regretful RSVPs.

While in Wales, one of Edward's knights was hit by an arrow fired from a longbow, a native weapon that shot missiles so hard and fast they could penetrate a church door. Edward was so impressed he hired Welsh bowmen to become the core of his army and the longbow would have a revolutionary impact, making the military power of the aristocratic cavalry obsolete.

Welsh tradition held that no man born on foreign soil could be prince, so the king of England swore that the new Prince of Wales would be Welsh-born, and would 'speak no English'—and promptly presented his baby Edward, recently born in Caernarfon.

Apparently, the Welsh lords found this funny. Edward became the first Prince of Wales, and since that day the first son of the monarch has held that title and been crowned in Caernarfon Castle. Sadly, the only problem with this story is that Edward's son did not take the title until he was sixteen, in 1301, although it's true that Long-shanks did take his heavily pregnant wife on campaign (strangely, this was quite common). It makes a nice story, but the next king to be crowned Prince of Wales in Caernarfon or anywhere in Wales was Edward Saxe-Coburg-Gotha, the future Edward VIII, in 1911.

The Welsh now found themselves subject to oppressive laws, forbidden to bear arms or even to entertain strangers overnight without permission from the authorities. For the next six hundred years, their language would be discouraged; yet, despite this, still utterly baffling to outsiders, it survives.

The Welsh war had cost a lot of money, and to raise more the king turned on an easier target. The Jews of England had arrived with William the Conqueror, and more came after most of them were burned out of the Norman capital Rouen. The sixteen thousand-strong community was never popular, but Edward lived in a time of increasing religious fanaticism, which had begun to ramp up first with the wars in the Holy Land and then in the thirteenth century with the Albigensian Crusade against the Cathar heresy in the south of France, which cost one million lives. Simon de Montfort had expelled all the Jews from Leicester, while the Church had also become noticeably more intolerant; the 1215 Lateran Council had for the first time insisted that Jews wear special markers on their clothes. Henry III, a credulous man with a double-digit IQ, was the first king to endorse the blood libel, the widely believed conspiracy theory that Jews were ritually murdering Christian boys.

Since Christians were banned from lending money and Jews were banned from doing almost everything else, this became their chosen profession, so that among the most prominent moneylenders were Jews, such as Aaron of Lincoln, Isaac 'the Russian' of

Hampshire, and Belaset of Wallingford, who also lent large amounts to the crown for projects such as Lincoln Cathedral. But this made Jews vulnerable to both embittered debtors and broke rulers.

Edward used a crackdown on counterfeiting as an opportunity to extract thirty-six thousand pounds from the Jewish population, and to execute over two hundred Jewish men on charges of forgery, as well as a number of Christians. In 1274, the king pushed through the Statute of Jewry, which stated: 'Each Jew, after he is seven years old, shall wear a distinguishing mark on his outer garment, in the form of two Tables joined, of yellow felt.' To modern ears this carries a somewhat sinister ring, although rules about clothing were widespread, and it wasn't only heretics, lepers, and prostitutes who had to wear special clothing (the latter were required to wear their clothes inside out) but each social class; in some countries, aristocrats had to wear fur by law, even in the sweltering heat.

After massacres at York and elsewhere by yokels who were enraged about something or other, Edward decreed that 'no [i]nquiries be made,' and in 1282 he began rounding up Jews and demanding payments for their release. Eight years later, he had the rest expelled, ensuring that many were robbed on their way to France and Flanders, and a large number were left to drown in the Thames. All in all, that invitation from Yad Vashem may take a while.

Incredibly, Edward's expulsion of the country's main financiers did not lead to the economic miracle he was hoping for and England's problems continued to get worse. Italians were brought in as replacement merchants, where they set up a banking community in Lombard Street in the City of London—which is still at the heart of the financial sector—not far from Old Jewry.[2] Their terms for the Latin units of currency, *lire, soldi,* and *denari,* from the Roman system, became the *£, s, d* of pre-decimal English currency, and survives as the symbol of the British pound.

The Welsh war of 1277 led Edward to borrow vast amounts from the Ricciardi of Lucca, one of Italy's major banking families, and by 1294 he was in hoc to the tune of four hundred thousand pounds. Always desperate for money, that same year he increased the tax on wool to two pounds a sack but backed down in 1297 after a revolt by leading lords who cited Magna Carta as legal grounds.

His reckless spending did, however, help to create the most important political institution in democratic history. English noblemen had first began having get-togethers they called 'parliament' as far as back as the 1230s, where they would sit around complaining about the king's French in-laws, but under Edward the original group of lords was joined by a second chamber. Longshanks called two 'parliaments' a year because he needed money, and in the 1270s the crown was in such desperate need of cash that it was decided that, because lords could not coerce the realm on their own and the consent of a larger group was needed, a second house of parliament was created, an assembly of knights that later became the House of Commons. (Soon afterwards, representatives of larger towns were invited to sit in the Commons alongside them.) Most of these early members of Parliament (MPs) were knights in the sense we imagine—84 percent of the 854 men in the parliamentary roll of arms in Edward II's reign did military service.

What followed was what many historians call a 'fiscal revolution,' which doesn't sound hugely exciting, but it had a huge impact on our lives. It meant that the Commons were required to vote through any money the king wanted to raise, so by the end of the fourteenth century the lawmaking body was firmly established.

King Edward confirmed parliamentary powers and enshrined Magna Carta into law within it, so his role in later creating English democracy is important, even if he did once threaten to hang a MP who disagreed with him. Most people, however, probably know him better as the bad guy in a classic Mel Gibson action film.

Chapter Three

Braveheart

Wales was relatively easy to defeat, but Edward then got embroiled in the far more complex politics of Scotland, which was another matter altogether. The northern kingdom was at that point absurdly violent, at every level of society. The border with England was inhabited by feuding clans who lived by cattle rustling and whose honor culture fed an unending cycle of revenge killings; considered a nuisance by both countries, many ended up being paid to live in Ulster and then onto the Appalachians. Further north were the even more terrifying Gaelic-speaking Highlanders, viewed as bandits by the lowland Scots, as well as various Viking throwbacks on the islands.

The northern English were terrified of the Scots, and occasionally a horde would pour over the border, attack some villages, and enslave a few locals, before inevitably collapsing into chaos. Then the English would head north with a massive army, burn everything in sight, and the Scots would simply hide until the invaders got hungry or bored.

Many people's knowledge of the Scottish Wars of Independence probably comes from *Braveheart*, a film in which the heroic William Wallace and Robert the Bruce are portrayed as regular fitba[1]-loving Scotsmen who only want freedom, while the English king is a sadistic, aristocratic proto-Nazi and his son an effete homosexual. In reality, Bruce was an Anglo-Norman nobleman who owned several estates in England and France, and like Edward spoke French as a first language (Edward most likely couldn't even speak English). Wallace was basically a criminal psychopath whose penchant for skinning people alive just happened to get caught up with the general violence of the time. Today he probably would have ended up in a high-security correctional facility sporting a tattoo on his eyeball.

Having said that, though *Braveheart* is possibly the most historically inaccurate film since the Messiah wore flares in *Jesus Christ Superstar*, Edward I was essentially your standard Hollywood English bad guy and his son was gay.[2]

Scottish history is complicated because a lot of its identity was made up in the nineteenth century by romantic novelists like Walter Scott and is now used to sell golfing holidays. The Kingdom of Scotland had developed from a merger of four different ethnic groups who, for various reasons, ended up at the edge of Europe; the Gaelic-speaking Scotti in the West, who had migrated from Ireland after the fall of Rome; the indigenous Picts of Caledonia in the North and East, who spoke a mysterious language that mixed Celtic and pre-Celtic words and got their name from their habit of painting their faces; the Britons of the southwest, who were related to the Welsh; and the Angles, who colonized the southeast of the country, which used to be part of the Kingdom of Northumbria. It was because of the Angles that the Scots came to speak a dialect of English, which became dominant after a large influx of English aristocrats following the Norman invasion. On top of this, the islands were also heavily settled by a fifth group, the Vikings, many of whom maintained a Scandinavian identity into quite recent times.

The first Pictish king to use the title King of Alba, or Scotland, was Kenneth MacAlpine in the ninth century, although some argue that accolade should go to his grandson Donald 'the Madman.' The most famous early Scottish monarch was Macbeth, although he was nothing like the Shakespearean character and was actually one of the few kings not to have murdered his predecessor; in the century before he ruled, five Scottish monarchs were assassinated and four were killed in battle. Macbeth, inevitably, went the same way.

England's and Scotland's aristocracies had been interlinked since the Norman conquest, when the remnants of the English royal family moved north and married into the House of Dunkeld. By Edward's time, nine out of thirteen Scottish earls held lands in England, while seven of their English equivalents owned property in Scotland.[3]

Like England, Scotland had a Norman ruling class, although bizarrely the Scots actually invited the Normans over as a sort of imported nobility, which many of those accustomed to the Normans must have regarded as unwise. Most of the Scottish barons, therefore, were basically French, including the great hero of independence Robert the Bruce (or le Brus, if you want to be strictly accurate). Bruce's grandfather had fought with Edward against de Montfort in his capacity as an English lord.

By Edward's time, Scotland had developed from being a very impoverished place—a century before it hadn't even had any cities—although compared to England, let alone France, it was still backwards. Culturally, it had become much more like England, too, and those in the south of the country, Lothian, basically saw themselves as English; they felt far more in common with people across the border, who spoke their language, than with the Gaels to the North. The town of Dryburgh, which today has a statue of William Wallace, was described at the time as being 'in the land of the English as well as the Scots.'

Scotland might well have been absorbed by its larger neighbor in the previous century had it not been for the war between John and the barons, and now Edward saw his chance to make it part of England—however, it only had the opposite effect of helping to create a Scottish identity, as there's nothing like a huge army rampaging through your lands to change how you see your neighbors.

The Wars of Independence began by chance. In 1286, Alexander III, King of Scots, was on his way back to spend his first night with his new young French wife Yolanda, and in his enthusiasm to get home in terrible weather rode his horse off a cliff by the Firth of Forth. His body was discovered in the morning.

Both his sons had already died, as had his daughter Margaret in childbirth, so his only heir was Margaret's two-year-old daughter by King Eric of Norway, another Margaret, called the 'Maid of Norway.' Alexander's first wife—confusingly, yet another Margaret—had been King Edward's sister, and so the ruling families were related. In fact, back in 1284 Alexander was the first to come up with the idea of a union of crowns, and for the Scottish royals the thought of becoming ruler of all Britain and getting to live in London obviously seemed like a great idea. However, in 1290 the then six-year-old Maid of Norway was on her way to her new kingdom when she died of seasickness in the Orkneys (people did actually die of seasickness; sea travel at the time was so dreadful people usually made wills before starting a voyage).

Edward was devastated, not because she was his great-niece, but because it scuppered his plans for her to marry his son Edward and therefore peacefully take over Scotland. It also threw the Scottish crown into chaos, with fourteen different men now claiming the throne.

That same year, King Edward was also slightly unhinged by his own wife's death. Queen Eleanor had been widely disliked for her rapaciousness, making a fortune cheaply by buying debt-ridden estates, and was 'high-handed and ruthless,' as one contemporary complained. She ended up very rich, so as the words to one popular song went: 'The king would like to get our gold/The queen, our manors fair, to hold.' And while most queens tended to bring out the merciful side of their men, she encouraged her husband to be more severe.[4] The chronicler of Dunstable Priory could only say of Eleanor upon her death that she was 'A Spaniard by birth' who had 'acquired many fine manors.' Which doesn't exactly suggest she was a national treasure.

For all his genuine grief, Edward turned his wife's death into something of a PR exercise, and had a cross built at every stop her body rested for its journey from Lincoln to London, twelve in total, and three of these Eleanor Crosses still survive.[5]

Meanwhile, the Scottish situation was getting incredibly confusing. As there were so many possible claimants to the throne, Edward insisted he be head of the selection process, an inquiry called 'the Great Cause,' which comprised eighty Scots and twenty-four Englishmen.

The two main contenders were John Balliol and Robert the Bruce, both great-great-great-grandsons of a previous king, David I. Balliol had the best claim, as his grandmother was the elder sister of Bruce's, and he was also essentially English, his father being lord of Barnard Castle in County Durham; this helped him in Edward's eyes, since Longshanks's main aim had been to 'reduce the king and kingdom of Scotland to his authority,' as he put it.

However, the inquiry ended up taking two years, prolonged after a third, sort of joke candidate entered, Floris of Holland (who Edward later had murdered for an unrelated reason). The whole thing went on so long that they had to have three adjournments before Edward chose Balliol on condition he recognize him as his overlord—a puppet. Balliol did not even dare call himself king in Edward's presence but 'your man of the realm of Scotland.'

Longshanks argued that English monarchs took precedent over Scottish ones because, according to Geoffrey Monmouth's fantastic account of early Britain, the country had been first inhabited by Trojans from modern-day Turkey, and the eldest son had founded modern-day England while the younger had settled to the North. Even at the time, the argument sounded rather tortured, and his real case was that he was strong and they were weak, and he had enormous catapults and they didn't. The Scots royal family were supposedly descended from Scota, a warrior princess daughter of a Pharaoh who captured the country from the family of Brutus—'Citation needed,' as a Wikipedia editor might put it.

Then in 1295, the French invaded Gascony and it all exploded again.

Relations between England and France had been stable for many years because Henry III and Louis IX had been married to two sisters. While Louis died on Crusade in 1270, his son Philippe III also enjoyed a good relationship with his cousin Edward I. He was called the Bold despite being famously indecisive, but, in 1285, he also passed away and was replaced by his son Philippe IV, or *Le Bel,* who was extremely ambitious as well as good-looking: 'The handsomest man in the world, [he] can do nothing but stare at men,' said one chronicler. This was because he was shy, I should add.

Philippe did see eye to eye with Edward on one thing—he expelled all the Jews from his country, too. Otherwise, though, they didn't really get on, as Philippe had his eyes on Gascony, and the two kings had previously argued. Back in 1291, Edward was supposed to arrange the marriage of his son Edward to Blanche, the king of France's sister. However, after hearing how beautiful she was he decided he wanted to marry her himself, so he sent his brother Edmund to sort it out. Philippe went back on the deal and Blanche was married off to a German while Longshanks instead got her younger sister Margaret. He was about sixty, she was maybe seventeen, and Edward was hugely excited about marrying the young French woman; her thoughts on the matter were not recorded but no doubt she was delighted.

Then, in 1294, while Balliol was being set up by Edward as his stooge, Philippe summoned the English king to do homage as his vassal for Gascony, a deliberately humiliating act. Edward dispatched his brother instead, and so in 1295 the French invaded Gascony and also raided Dover. Edward ranted: 'the king of France, not satisfied with the treacherous invasion of Gascony, has prepared a mighty fleet and army, for the purpose of invading England and wiping the English tongue from the face of the earth.'

As a puppet, John Balliol had proposed a tax on the Scots to pay for the English to fight the French, which obviously went down like a lead balloon. The Scottish Council of Nobles furiously rejected Edward's demand for military help. Instead, Balliol began a very ineffective uprising against England, before quickly backing down again.

The English king marched north and besieged Berwick just inside Scotland, demanding the town's surrender; the locals bared their buttocks at him, which considering they had very meager defenses, was not a good idea. The king was busy knighting some soldiers when the English navy began to attack and so he was forced to start the battle early. Afterwards, he massacred several hundred of the eleven thousand population, but in an act of woolly liberalism, he allowed the garrison of two hundred to surrender, expelled the remaining population, and burned down the city. Either soon before or soon after, depending on who you believe, the Scots raided nearby Corbridge and slaughtered two hundred English civilians.

Edward had Berwick rebuilt, wheeling the first barrow of earth himself, true to his gritty image. He enjoyed the all-round toughness of soldiering and would sleep out in the cold with the troops on campaign when, in December 1294, now a grizzled fifty-five-year-old, he besieged Conwy in north Wales and found himself cut off by floods, the king divided up his wine with his soldiers and refused to have more than his share of rations.

After marching into Scotland, Edward took to London the Stone of Scone, the traditional rock of Scottish kingship that was supposed to have been brought from Ireland by the first Scots kings, and he installed another puppet ruler in Balliol's place. Edward judged Balliol as in contempt of court and sentenced him to lose three castles and towns: 'Like a lamb amongst wolves,' one contemporary described him.

Edward now went on a tour of Scotland, getting as far as Elgin, which was further than any English king had ever been. The difficult part, however, was not in defeating the Scots but in running the place, the governor of Scotland being an especially unsought-after job. The Earl of Surrey, the man who Edward had forced to administer the country, was in a matter of months desperately trying to palm it off to others. He spent most of his time in the north of England as he couldn't bear the Scottish weather, which is relentlessly dismal (not that England is exactly Hawaii).

As for Balliol, he embraced the chance to retire in England where he'd 'dwell there in the ways that used to be his, and would hunt in his parks, and do what he wished for his solace and pleasure.' However, before he quit, Edward decided to humiliate him with an act of ceremonial 'degradation' at Montrose in which the Lion of Scotland was ripped from his surcoat, or tabard, earning him the nickname Toom (empty) Tabard.

Edward wanted to build lots of castles in Scotland as he had in Wales, but they had run out of money and could only afford wood by that point. In fact, between 1294 and 1304, the king spent a million pounds on war, a vast fortune at the time that led to widespread discontent (as a rough estimate, one pound then corresponds to $1,000 in today's money, although changes in the cost of living make such conversions inexact). In 1297, there was open revolt by the aristocracy and so, in response, Edward reissued what turned out to be the final, definite Magna Carta, establishing certain fundamental freedoms under English law such as the right to not be arrested without charge.

However, in order to raise money for a Crusade in the Holy Land—still his lifelong goal—Edward sent agents to raid people's savings, including eleven thousand pounds taken from private deposits. They forced their way into ecclesiastical buildings with axes and smashed up chests. When the elderly Dean of St. Paul went to deliver the clergy's response, he collapsed and died in terror at having to confront the king. Not one to tread on people's sensibilities, Edward still sent knights to the dead man's colleagues saying he would have their money or they would be in trouble. He ended up outlawing the clergy en masse after they refused to hand over cash, with royal agents taking their food and livestock. When Roger Bigod in Parliament in 1297 questioned why he should have to help fight Edward's wars, the king replied 'Either you will go or you will hang' to a stunned assembly.

King Edward also tried to recover crown lands that had been lost during the reign of his father with a new scheme called *Quo Warranto*, 'by what right,' whereby royal officials would turn up at people's homes and demand to know by what right they owned the land. The Earl of Gloucester,[6] when asked this question, famously showed them his big sword and shouted 'Behold, my lords. This warrant. For my ancestors came with William the Bastard and conquered their lands with the swords—and by the sword I shall defend them from anyone wishing to seize them.' Which they took as a reasonable answer.

In 1299, a truce between England and France was agreed upon, by which the king would marry Princess Margaret and his son Edward would marry her sister Isabella, all of which seems a bit weird. However, there soon emerged yet another Scottish uprising, and another mass of mad-looking people crossed the border and terrorized the north of England. As Walter of Guisborough put it: 'In all the monasteries and churches between Newcastle and Carlisle the service of God totally ceased, for all the canons, monks, and priests fled before the Scots, as did nearly all the people.'

Edward called his barons to join him in another assault, but many refused because he had milked them for so much money, and so his invasion force of Scotland in 1298 was mostly Welsh, Irish, and Gascon. It was hard to get English knights to go to Scotland because there was almost nothing to steal; Edward I even offered to pay knights for military service in 1282, but they refused, perhaps seeing it as an insult.

A new figure emerged at this point. In 1296, there had been a court reference to one 'William le Waleys, a thief,' but the great Scottish leader is first mentioned by English chroniclers the following year when they describe him as 'a chief of brigands' and 'a vagrant and a fugitive.'

William Wallace, as fans of *Braveheart* will know, became involved because the local English sheriff killed his wife, although what the film didn't mention is that this was in revenge for Wallace murdering the sheriff's son because he had offended Wallace by making a disparaging comment about his clothes. According to another story, Wallace also got into a fatal fight when an English soldier said: 'What's a Scot need a knife like that, as the monk said who last screwed your wife?' Wallace also had an English treasurer called Cressingham skinned and turned into a belt, on top of many other atrocities, so he was not quite the romantic figure many would like to believe. Wallace 'adhered to no rules of chivalry, but waged total war against man, woman, and child,' as one chronicler put it.

Being from a gentry family, Wallace wouldn't have painted himself blue in the ancient Pictish style any more than the commander-in-chief of Her Majesty's Armed Forces would walk around today dressed as a Tudor minstrel.[7] Much of the Wallace story, including an early form of the subplot where Longshanks's second wife falls for Wallace, comes from a poet called 'Blind Harry' who lived two hundreds year later, hardly the kind of testimony that would stand up in court.

The invasion was a disaster to start with. Drunken fighting between English and Welsh infantrymen led the latter to withdraw and then threaten to side with the Scots. Edward replied, sounding rather like Grand Moff Tarkin ordering the destruction of a planet in *Star Wars*: 'Who cares if our enemies joined together? We shall beat them both in a day.'

With Wallace leading the rebellion, other noblemen now joined in, including the powerful barons, James Stewart and William

Douglas. (Douglas had married his wife by simply kidnapping her, one of the exciting ancient Scandinavian traditions that hadn't entirely died out in the area.)

In September 1297, the Scots won a rare victory at Stirling Bridge, which was only wide enough for men in two-by-two formation. However, after some initial heroism and glory, the Scots always lose these wars, and the following year at Falkirk, the inevitable happened. The Scots were on the side of a hill in a hedgehog formation and realizing they could not win, their nobles fled the field. For the battle, Edward had large new windows put in the queen's chambers nearby so 'she and her ladies could observe their gallant menfolk in action,' this being medieval men's idea of what women found attractive.[8]

The English were helped in this conflict by enormous siege machines that had to be dragged by several thousand men and that could lob huge amounts of artillery at the enemy. One of these trebuchets, 'the War Wolf,' especially excited King Edward, and he even refused a surrender because he wanted to try out his new toy. (Trebuchets often had scary names, such as 'God's Stone Thrower' or 'the Furious.') The Scots, meanwhile, had to rely on more low-tech but equally gruesome tricks, one of which was to trap English soldiers on a bridge, knock the bridge down, and leave the soldiers to drown in their armor.

Even the King of England was almost killed at one point when a crossbow bolt went through his clothes while he was riding around the walls; on another occasion, stones from a catapult scared his horse, which threw him.

While a war of independence was going on, many Scots were also engaged in ongoing feuds with other Scots, and Wallace was eventually captured by a Scottish nobleman and was handed over to the English in 1305, then taken to London where he was tried for treason. Obviously, he wasn't going to be found Not Guilty and was soon hanged, drawn, and quartered near what is now the city's fashionable Smithfield Market, having first been dragged naked through the streets. He was also castrated before having his stomach cut open and his bowels burned before him.

Wallace's body was taken to the four corners not just of England but of Britain, and his head was stuck on a pike in London. The Great Seal of Scotland, the symbol of authority and law in that country, was then presented to the king who threw it to one side, musing philosophically, 'A man does good business when he rids himself of a turd.'

But while Wallace was dead, he had the last laugh; soon after the release of Mel Gibson's film in 1995, John Major's despised government sent the Stone of Scone back up to Scotland in a desperate attempt to make the Conservative Party less hated there (it didn't work—the following year they lost all their seats at the General Election).

But now came the moment for another Scottish hero, Robert the Bruce. Bruce was no angel either, and the Church refused to support his Scottish independence struggle because he'd murdered a rival in church. This occurred in February 1306, before the high altar of the Franciscan church at Dumfries where Bruce stabbed to death John Comyn of Badenoch, former guardian of Scotland, and had himself declared king. In response, Robert's sister Mary Bruce and another woman, the Countess of Buchan, who had crowned Robert, were taken prisoner and stuck in wooden cages by Edward. They were lucky; any man who supported Robert was executed, including three brothers and three brothers-in-law.

Longshanks also began to execute Scottish noblemen. John of Athollwas the first earl put to death by an English king since 1076, something considered against the rules of chivalry. He did at least give Atholl a special exemption in that he was hanged on gallows thirty feet higher than his fellow, common prisoners, after which he was beheaded and burned. (It's important in Britain to have these class distinctions, even during executions.) He then had Bruce's

sister-in-law Isabella, Countess of Buchan, stuck in a cage for partici-
pating at his coronation. Edward had begun a spiral of brutalization
in Britain that reached its nadir the following century with the War
of the Roses, but it was partly because he was more concerned with
the idea of law. He saw people rebelling against him not as rival
warlords, as his ancestors might have done, but as traitors.

On the run from his enemies, both English and Scottish, Robert the Bruce now realized his only hope was to present himself as
an anti-English independence leader. At one point, in perhaps the
most famous incident of the Wars of Independence, Bruce was hiding in a cave and, while there, watched a spider attempt to attach
a thread to a beam, failing to do so six times. The spider stuck at
it and achieved it the seventh time around, and this inspired Bruce
to persevere.[9]

And so with a fresh Scottish revolt in 1306, Edward, now sixty-
eight, marched north once again, vowing he would not sleep two
nights in the same place until the rebels were defeated. Before setting off, he held a Whit Sunday banquet at Westminster Abbey,
known since as The Feast of Swans. Here he bestowed knighthood
on his son Edward and three hundred other young men; the king
swore two oaths, one to avenge himself of Robert the Bruce and the
other to go on Crusade—which at his age must have looked pretty
unlikely. The king's son then swore he would not sleep two nights
in the same place until he had followed his father's mission to crush
the Scots, and all the other young knights swore to follow him. The
younger Edward, who preferred basket weaving to fighting, clearly
had no intention of doing this, and such oaths were often made at
feasts where people had drunk a lot. Various chronicles from the
Crusades record men swearing to go to Jerusalem while hopelessly
drunk then waking up terrified.

After this lavish ceremony, a grand tournament was held to cele-
brate the future king and his glorious rule (with two fatalities, which
wasn't especially bad for sporting events in the period).

However, near the border, Longshanks came down with dysentery and died; according to popular legend, even with his dying breath the king demanded that servants carry his bones around Scotland, having boiled them down, until the rebels were crushed. Sadly this probably isn't true.

Edward's death was kept a secret for a fortnight and anyone who talked about it was imprisoned, but when the public learned of it there was great sorrow; as was always the case in medieval Europe, people liked to be ruled by a strong man, even a cruel and oppressive one who treated them terribly. One writer lamented that Edward had outshined 'not only Arthur and Alexander but also Brutus, Solomon, and Richard the Lionheart,' adding, 'We should perceive him to surpass all the kings of the earth who came before him.' A Westminster obituary writer said Edward was peaceable to the obedient 'but to the sons of pride he was indeed "a terrible king."' His gravestone in Westminster reads: 'Edward the First, Hammer of the Scots. Keep Faith.' There was no effigy, perhaps on his son's orders; the two did not like each other.

There were some good aspects to the king. He was very well traveled for the time, having gone all over Western Europe, North Africa, and Cyprus, although to be fair these were almost entirely for battles. Edward also commissioned surveys of England that led to the first maps being made of the country, and before then there was almost no geographical knowledge in Western Europe; however, his motivation was probably less wonderment at the world and more a desire to invade the places on the map.

The same could be said for the other main development of his reign: Parliament. Because his wars were so relentlessly expensive, he was forced to give more and more say to the Lords and Commons. The Gascony crisis of 1294–1303, in the words of one historian, led to the 'creation of state finances by parliamentary taxation.'[10] In essence, he created Parliament as we know it, even if this wasn't necessarily his intention.

CHAPTER FOUR

Famine

An Unconventional King

Had it not been for the relentless tragedy of fourteenth-century life, Edward I would have been followed by Alfonso I. But his eldest son passed away before him, joining a list of unlikely sounding English kings who died before their time, among them Eustace, Arthur, Frederick, and Ralph (nephew of Edward the Confessor who, had he not died in 1057, may well have inherited the throne a decade later).

Instead, the crown passed to his only surviving son, Edward, who, though tall, blond, and athletic, would be a grave disappointment to his father. Edward II spent most of his time with handsome court 'favorites,' a medieval version of the gossip column's 'pop star and close friend,' and preferred basket weaving, thatching, gardening, and other early forms of DIY to soldiering, which in the rather unenlightened minds of the average medieval person were seen as unworthy of a king. But the most undignified of his pursuits was rowing, since no king should ever need to pick up an oar, in the same way as a gangster might lose respect if he turned up to a crime family meeting on a bicycle wearing a helmet.

Edward II was also into amateur dramatics and a 'minstrel fanatic,' which might have had something to do with the fact that he was raised by a nurse who was also a part-time minstrel; at his coronation, he paid for 154 musicians to play. On one occasion, the king gave 'Jack of St. Albans' fifty shillings because 'he danced before the king on a table and made him laugh very greatly.' Edward also paid a cook twenty shillings 'because he rode before the King . . . and often fell from his horse,' which also made the king laugh 'very greatly'—snippets that suggest he wasn't a great intellectual titan. He also lost a lot of money in betting and playing pitch-and-toss.

People often complained that King Edward's countenance was unregal, that he preferred gardening to soldiering and liked to mingle with 'harlots and jesters.' He also enjoyed the company of 'mechanicals' and 'buffoons, singers, actors, carters, ditchers, oarsmen, and sailors,' according to a contemporary chronicler, Ranulf Higden.

Most controversially of all, he liked to swim, which was considered not just unmanly, but actually sinister to the medieval mind, 'the spooky embrace of an unnatural element.'[1] Even sailors and fishermen considered it bad luck to learn to swim and, unsurprisingly, a lot of them drowned. In February 1303, it was recorded that the king had gone swimming with 'Robert the Fool,' mixing his two favorite pastimes. He wasn't totally uncultured, however, and he was the first English monarch to found a college: King's Hall, Cambridge.

Edward II's reign would begin disastrously, and would only get worse. According to one historian, he was 'arguably the worst and ultimately the most dangerous king ever to rule England.'[2] Another described him as 'one of the best examples of the brutal and brainless athletes who ended up on the throne.'[3]

Edward was cursed with having poor judgment in people, most likely a result of his lonely, sad childhood. He was the youngest of sixteen, and almost all of his siblings were either far older or deader than him; his mother passed away when he was only six and his father was away for most of his childhood starting wars, hardly the best environment to raise a child. Longshanks was certainly not from the hugs-and-kisses school of parenting, being prone to boxing children on the ear when they annoyed him; as well as throwing his daughter's crown in a fire, he once ripped Edward II's hair out in a rage. The cause was Piers Gaveston.

Gaveston was a minor nobleman from Gascony, and had been Edward's friend from a young age; their relationship was intimate and most likely sexual. It was Longshanks who had selected Gaveston as a companion for his son, and when the king took them campaigning in Scotland they hung around each other all the time, so much so that the court chroniclers compared them to David and Jonathan, 'the great biblical example of friendship between two men,' although the Old Testament prophets probably wouldn't have entirely approved of their relationship.

However, it was noted by a London chronicler that a year before his death, the old king 'saw that his son, the Prince of Wales, had an inordinate love for a certain Gascon knight,' and lost his temper a bit. When Edward II asked his father to give the county of Ponthieu in northern France to Gaveston, which young Edward owned through his mother, he replied: 'You bastard son of a bitch! Now you want to give lands away—you who never gained any? As the Lord lives, were it not for fear of breaking up the kingdom, you should never enjoy your inheritance.'

Late in 1306, Gaveston had deserted the king's campaign in Scotland along with twenty-one other young knights to go to a tournament. He was pardoned in January 1307, but then a month later was banished from England and banned from returning without permission from the king. Before he left, young Edward gave Piers two tourneying outfits in green emblazed with Gaveston's coat of arms; one in fine linen, the other in velvet embroidered with pearls and piping of silver and gold. Not something that male friends normally do for each other.

So when the old king died, Edward immediately recalled his favorite and had him made Earl of Cornwall before his father was even buried. Five days after the funeral, he had Piers married to his niece Margaret, with the new monarch guest of honor at Berkhamsted Castle for the marriage ceremony. He even paid for the bride and groom to be showered with silver pennies.

Edward kept a chamber for Gaveston close to his own, and six months into his reign made him 'keeper of the realm.' The two men even wore the same clothes when they were holding court. Their relationship soon caused tremendous resentment among the nobility, not necessarily because it was sexual, but because of the favoritism and the perks his 'minion' was getting, perks historically owned by the leading noble families. Gaveston also seemed to have that great gift of annoying everyone and, to make matter worse, he was also a foreigner and fairly lowborn, being from a minor noble family.

But no one was angrier at the relationship than Edward's new wife Isabella, the strong-willed and highly intelligent twelve-year-old daughter of Philippe of France. Just a month after Edward and Isabella's marriage came the disastrous coronation, wherein Edward displayed a coat of arms representing himself and Gaveston, and sat with the man instead of his new wife throughout the celebration. By the end of 1308, the leading lords were demanding Edward get rid of the Gascon. Gaveston's arrogance was 'intolerable to the barons, and a prime cause of hatred and rancour'; he made enemies by giving powerful barons bitchy nicknames, such as 'whoreson' for the Earl of Gloucester, 'the fiddler' for the Earl of Leicester, and 'the black hound' for Warwick. 'Let him call me hound,' Warwick told his allies, 'one day the hound will bite him.'

The barons were further infuriated because Gaveston was also a brilliant fighter, holding tournaments where he beat everyone in sight. Later that year, a number of noblemen asked the king to remove Gaveston, so Edward made him Regent of Ireland, where he did a terrible job, but he soon returned uninvited. With the war in Scotland being lost, a group of barons—led by the king's fantastically rich cousin Thomas, Earl of Lancaster, a man with a private army larger than the king's—set up a committee called the Lords Ordainers, and demanded reform of the Crown.

In February 1310, a group of lords arrived at Parliament armed and angry. The king was forced to give into their demand that he appoint a body of twenty-one Ordainers, lords who would 'ordain and establish the estate of our household and of our realm.' The rebels stated that 'unless the king granted their demands, they would not have him for king, nor keep the fealty that they had sworn to him.'

To distract from all his problems, Edward decided to invade Scotland and take Gaveston with him, forcing Queen Isabella, still only fifteen, to come along. It didn't go well. Most of the earls wouldn't join them, while Robert the Bruce wouldn't play by the established rules of war by meeting the English on open ground, but instead conducted guerrilla fighting. In the end, Edward spent eight futile months at Berwick getting nowhere, and so he and Isabella rode south in July 1311.

While Gaveston stayed as the king's lieutenant in Scotland, Edward returned to be confronted by forty-one fresh demands from the Lords Ordainers. Some of these reflected the growing importance of Parliament and its evolution into a check on royal power: they demanded that the lords in Parliament were to be king's advisers with the power to vet all royal appointments; that the king could only wage war with baronial consent; that Parliament must have more say in financial matters; and that all revenue must be paid into the treasury all important and serious issues that have some bearing on politics today. Their main concern, however, was that he get rid of Gaveston.

Edward protested that they 'stop persecuting my brother Piers,' but he eventually agreed and the Earl of Cornwall was exiled in November 1311, for the third time. However, at Christmas, in a soap-opera like scene, Gaveston turned up in England yet again, and the following month he was with the king in York. The rebellion stepped up now.

In February 1311, the leading critical baron, Henry Lacy, Earl of Lincoln, had died; he had been a force for moderation, and with him gone, leadership of the opposition passed to his son-in-law, Thomas of Lancaster. Lancaster was the son of Edward I's brother Edmund, held huge amounts of land in the North, had an enormous private army, and was 'acutely conscious of his own preeminent position among the English nobility, set apart as he was from his peers both by birth and by the scale of his wealth and power.'[4] As well as being the cousin of Edward II, he was also the uncle of Isabella, his mother having been the granddaughter of Louis VIII. He already owned large areas of Lancashire, Leicester, and Derby, and his marriage to the heiress Alice Lacy meant he also got Lincoln and Salisbury, too. He was 'a loner, aloof and haughty,' and did not get on with the other opponents of the king, their only bond being a shared hatred of Gaveston.

By this stage, the queen hated Gaveston so much that her father Philippe IV paid two earls to plot against him after Isabella complained of his behavior, but he withdrew after she was given the county of Ponthieu by her husband.

While Edward and his lover were on the border, the rebel lords marched north to confront them, improbably claiming they were only heading up to a tournament, and just happened to have a really large army with them. At the end of April, Lancaster arrived at Newcastle and Edward fled by sea with Gaveston, leaving weapons, jewels, and horses behind, as well as his now-pregnant wife. This was the first of two occasions in which he'd deserted Isabella, but in fairness to Edward the sea journey would have been too dangerous for her unborn child. She also had nothing to fear if captured, unlike Gaveston; as it was, the two men spent a miserable five-day voyage in rough seas, which must have been especially grim for Piers as he had recently been ill.

Edward was hopeless as king, but no historian has anything nice to say about the 'mediocrities' opposed to him:[5] Lancaster was 'sulky, vindictive, self-seeking, brutal, and vicious,' the Earl of Warwick was 'treacherous,' and another malcontent, Seward de Warenne, the Earl of Surrey, was 'a disreputable nonentity.' Warwick in particular had that very Renaissance combination of being both very interested in high culture and literature, and also a cruel sadist.[6]

Gaveston would soon experience this firsthand. He was besieged in Scarborough and surrendered to the Earl of Pembroke, a critical but loyal supporter of the crown who swore to take care of his prisoner. However, when Pembroke went away to see his wife Beatrice, Warwick, knowing that Gaveston was unguarded, assembled an army and rode the twenty-five miles to Pembroke's Castle, in Deddington. Pembroke's soldiers laid down their arms and Warwick shouted from outside his windows: 'Get up traitor—you are taken.'[7] The poor man was 'led forth not as an earl but as a thief' and, on June 19, was handed over to Lancaster's men and dragged two miles to Blacklow Hill, first on foot at the end of a rope and then by an old horse. Finally, on Lancaster's orders, a soldier stabbed Gaveston and, as he fell, another took a sword out and chopped off his head. The Earl of Cornwall's body was left to rot in a field and was eventually rescued by monks.

According to a chronicler, the killers 'knew that when the matter came to the king's notice, he would, if he could, proceed to take vengeance.'[8] Naturally, Edward was devastated, and on the anniversary of his lover's death he traveled to France to be entertained by 'Bernard the Fool and fifty-four naked dancers.' We all get through these things in our own way.

A few months later, the queen gave birth to a son, which her family insisted on calling Louis, but which the English lords vetoed in favor of Edward; Londoners who just weeks earlier feared their city would be caught up in a civil war partied in the streets with free wine, which was always given out during such events, and which inevitably led to multiple casualties.

The royal couple soon headed for France, where things might have appeared all in order to observers; Edward and Isabella over-slept for one event and the French hosts indulgently let them be, assuming it was down to Edward wanting to stay in bed with a beautiful wife, probably making ze sweet love. Which was probably unlikely.[9] In July, the lords had assembled in London and had to wait while the king didn't appear or even send word.

Bannockburn

To turn attention away from his incompetence, Edward invaded Scotland in 1314, managing to suffer one of the most humiliating defeats in English history. The battle of Bannockburn, in which Robert the Bruce's men were outnumbered two-to-one by the English, was fought in 'an evil, deep, and wet marsh' and, while the terrain didn't help, Edward's disastrous leadership was mostly to blame. Two leading noblemen, the Earls of Hereford and Gloucester, had bickered over who would lead, and the king dithered, offering them joint command. Eventually, Gloucester was so full of rage he decided to win the argument by single-handedly charging at the Scots. He was hacked to death instantly, which at least resolved the question of who was in charge.

In the ensuing battle, some one thousand Englishmen were killed, among them twenty-two barons and sixty-eight knights, and more lost their lives in the fifty-mile pursuit that followed. To cap the disaster, the Privy Seal, the highly symbolic personal insignia of the monarch, was also taken. The Scots lost just two knights and five hundred pike men, having used low-tech skills to beat a more advanced enemy, digging and then covering up holes around the English lines, into which many fell.

Edward fled back south, lucky to escape with his life, after which years of raids continued in northern England, and at one point one-fifth of the country was paying tribute to the Scottish king.

Meanwhile Robert's brother, Edward Bruce, invaded Ireland and declared himself king there.

Then the crops failed. Europe was becoming much colder after four warm centuries, during which London enjoyed the same climate as central France today; wine production in England ended in 1250 and would not return for centuries, while cereal growing retreated in Scandinavia and the European colony in Greenland was abandoned to its fate.[10]

The changing weather was the major factor in a wider economic depression linked to wars in Asia Minor in the 1250s and in France in the 1290s. Back in 1289, a great storm ruined the harvest, and, in 1309–1310, the Thames froze, while the Baltic turned to ice twice that decade. There had been five famines in England between 1272 and 1311, but 'between 1315 and 1319 came a crescendo of calamity.'[11]

Johannes de Trokelowe, a Benedictine monk at the time, wrote: 'In the year of our Lord 1315, apart from the other hardships with which England was afflicted, hunger grew in the land . . . Meat and eggs began to run out, capons and fowl could hardly be found, animals died of pest, swine could not be fed because of the excessive price of fodder . . . The land was so oppressed with want that when the king came to St. Albans on the feast of St. Laurence [10 August] it was hardly possible to find bread on sale to supply his immediate household.'

The lack of sun also hindered the production of salt, which made meat preservation harder, while many animals drowned in the floods, which also increased the number of parasites and crop diseases. There was misery 'such as our age has never seen,' and people were reduced to digging up the newly buried to eat, while in Poland it was reported that starving peasants had been taking down hanged men from gibbets. According to one chronicler, the poor ate 'dogs, cats, the dung of doves, even their own children.'

At least the Great Famine also killed any hopes of a great Celtic alliance against England. The Scots had invaded Ireland to 'liberate' it, and though there may have been some good intentions somewhere, these disappeared as their soldiers became so hungry that they even dug up fresh graves. Native churchmen complained that the Scots were even worse than the English, and they 'left neither wood nor lea, nor corn nor crop nor stead nor barn nor church, but fired and burnt them all.' Ireland's Anglo-Norman elite had more in common with the native Irish than the French-speaking Bruces; many Anglo-Irish had become 'degenerates,' as the English described it, adopting the Irish language, law, and custom.[12]

There was also a huge increase in crime back in England, which was already absurdly violent by today's standards. In fact, government attempts to fight crime were often resented by civic leaders, many of whom were at least responsible for some of the violence, so that when Edward I introduced a crackdown in 1304, 'a contemporary songsmith who purported to be a war veteran complained that, as a result of the new measures, good men like himself were being falsely accused and unjustly imprisoned, simply because they had knocked their servants about a bit.'[13]

Edward II's reign was so violent the country was terrorized by heavily armed middle-class gangs known as 'trail bastons,' the worst being the Folvilles, a Leicestershire gentry family who for a decade committed numerous murders, rapes, and robberies near to their home of Ashby Folville, called the 'Castle of the Four Winders.' In 1326, they killed a senior tax collector and, in 1332, kidnapped and ransomed a royal judge, Sir Richard Willoughby. Along with another criminal gang, the Coterel brothers, they made life a misery for people in large areas of Nottinghamshire and Derbyshire.

However, the judge in question was largely hated and the gang was popular with the sort of people who always idolize violent outlaws; 'Folville's Law' became used as a term to mean robbery of someone who probably deserved it. As the old joke goes, they were halfway to becoming Robin Hood—stealing from the rich, without getting around to giving it to the poor.

Many criminals came to horrific ends: Richard Folville, a vicar of all things, was eventually dragged away from church by armed men and beheaded. However, many outlaws eventually received pardons after fighting in the English army in Scotland or France, among them at least two of Friar Richard's brothers, as well as notorious outlaws such as Sir William de Chetulton and Sir John de Legh, and another gang leader, James Stafford.

This was a period where violence was far more common than today, and from unlikely sources. Among the most notorious priest gangs were the clergy from Lichfield Cathedral who helped the Coterel brothers on occasion, while on October 18, 1327, the monks of Bury St. Edmunds went to the nearby parish church where they burst in with armor and seized several citizens. When townsfolk went to the abbey to demand their release, the monks replied with missiles, killing many people. A large army was summoned, which included twenty-eight chaplains, and the abbey was set alight and stormed.

Historian Barbara Hanawalt recalled one incident in Northamptonshire when 'a certain William of Wellington, parish chaplain of *Yelvertoft*, sent John, his clerk, to John Cobbler's house to buy a candle for him for a penny. But John would not send it to him without the money wherefore William became enraged, and, knocking in the door upon him, he struck John in the front part of the head so that his brains flowed forth and he died forthwith.'

The homicide rate in England was at least ten times what it is today, with London having a higher murder level than the most dangerous American cities in the early twenty-first century; the vast majority of murderers escaped justice, although if they were caught the punishment was gruesome. While today the poor are far more likely to be the victims and perpetrators of violence, the opposite was true in the fourteenth and fifteenth centuries, when some 26 percent of male English aristocrats died from violence, compared to roughly 0.4 percent of American men today.[14]

Almost every area of life was more violent. Popular sports at the time consisted of events in which 'players with hands tied behind them competed to kill a cat nailed to a post by battering it to the death with their heads, at the risk of cheeks ripped open or eyes scratched out by the frantic animal's claws'; alternatively men would beat to death a pig in a pen with clubs 'to the laughter of spectators.'[15] Everyone considered this great fun, accompanied by the sound of trumpeters playing in the background.

The most popular form of entertainment at the time were religious 'mystery' plays, which featured scenes from the Bible played out by actors, but were far more like an HBO series than Golden Age Hollywood. When John the Baptist was decapitated, 'the actor was whisked away so cunningly in exchange for a fake corpse and fake head spilling ox blood that the audience shrieked in excitement.'[16] A man playing Jesus would be tied to the cross for three hours reciting verse, often in agony.

Religious plays were put together by the various guilds of each city, comprising the different trades, and often ended in mass brawls between actors. At Chester in 1399, there was a running battle between weavers and fullers during the procession; twenty years later at York, carpenters and shoemakers attacked skinners, using clubs and axes. At Newcastle, laws were introduced against 'the dissension and discord that hath been amongst the Crafts of the said Towne as of man slaughter and murder and other mischiefs.'

This violence went right to the top, and increased after the death of Gaveston, when Edward's behavior became increasingly bizarre. In 1317, he came under the spell of Nicholas of Wisbech, a fraudulent friar who claimed to own a vial of holy oil given to Thomas Becket; the king believed that if he were re-anointed with this oil, all the political troubles in England would end and he would also be able to conquer the Holy Land. The pope said no.

In 1318, a lunatic cleric called John Powderham turned up at Beaumont Palace in Oxford claiming to be the rightful son of Edward I. He argued that the so-called monarch was in reality a carter's son and they had been mixed up as babies. He was clearly mad, and the king thought of keeping him as a fool. Today, Powderham would probably have a popular blog revealing the 'real truth' the mainstream media would be too biased to reveal. However, people were unhappy enough with the monarch to entertain the idea that maybe Powderham was onto something, so the king had him hanged. During his trial, the poor man claimed that his pet cat was possessed and had incited him, so the cat was hanged, too. The execution of this madman infuriated the queen 'beyond words'; there were already signs of a deep problem with their marriage. (Isabella had a charitable side, once ensuring that a Scottish orphan boy she met on the road was given new clothes and sent to London to be taught and given medical help for the disease of the scalp from which he was suffering.)

In the meantime, the opposition was weakened by various mutual hatreds. The Earl of Surrey had been in a loveless and childless marriage to Jeanne of Bar, the king's niece, and for a number of years had wanted to marry his mistress, with whom he already had two sons. He and Lancaster did not get on, and so Lancaster supported the Church's refusal to grant an annulment. In retaliation, Surrey abducted Lancaster's wife, Alice Lacy. They also had an unhappy marriage, so she may have colluded in the stunt, and this public humiliation led to a private war between the two men.

The only thing that united them was a hatred of the court favorite, and luckily, after the fall of Gaveston, Edward adopted a new, even worse one, Hugh Despenser the Younger, along with his father Hugh Despenser the Elder. Despenser the Younger was 'a menacing predator, as opposed to Gaveston's distracting peacock,'[17] and was notorious for having murdered a captive, Llewelyn Bren, in horrific fashion, after he had surrendered. Despenser was greedy and ruthless, and, having married the king's niece Eleanor, was intent on increasing his power base in the West; he tried to grab land owned by a Marcher family on the Welsh border, the once mighty de Briouzes, and also alienated Roger Mortimer, the leading magnate in the region. While the country was suffering famine, the younger Despenser was putting vast amounts of gold into banks in Florence. The queen disliked the Despensers intensely, and on her knees she begged her husband to get rid of them, but to no avail.

In the spring of 1321, Marcher lords led by Roger Mortimer mobilized for a meeting in Yorkshire with Lancaster and other northern barons. Parliament was surrounded by the armed retainers of the barons, and the Despensers were banished. The younger Despenser became a pirate.

Lancaster tried to go into alliance with Robert the Bruce, but Bruce didn't trust him, partly because Lancaster kept referring to himself as 'King Arthur' during negotiations, which made the Scotsman suspect he wasn't entirely well.

Briefly, Edward's luck changed and he seemed to turn everything around. He defeated a rebellion by Mortimer, with the help of the Welsh, and Despenser, now back on land, captured Thomas of Lancaster in Yorkshire. The king's cousin was put on trial in a kangaroo court and was soon found guilty. Edward agreed he should be spared hanging in tribute to his royal blood so, at Pontefract in Yorkshire in March 1322, his head was cut off. Dressed in rags and wearing a ripped hat, Lancaster was bundled onto an old mare and forced to ride to his execution in sleet while locals pelted him with snowballs before being forced to kneel, facing Scotland, which he was accused of conspiring with. He was killed with 'two or three clumsy strokes' until eventually his head came off, the first member of the royal family to be executed since the Norman conquest.

This was followed a week later by the murder of six leading Lancastrians, among them John Mowbray who was hanged at York on March 2, and another rebel, Bartholomew Badlesmere, who was dragged through Canterbury by horses and taken to a crossroads where he was hanged and decapitated.

Dozens were sent to prison, among them Alice Lay, Lancaster's widow, who was told she would be burned to death unless she gave most of her possessions to Despenser and his father. Mortimer was condemned to be executed, but this was commuted to being locked up in the Tower, in quarters that were 'less elegant than they were seemly.'

The 'judicial murder' of Lancaster shocked the country and a cult soon grew around his tomb in Pontefract Priory, where it was said that a drowned child returned to life and a blind priest had his sight restored. To mock this, a servant of Hugh Despenser defecated on the same spot, but it was said—the medieval chronicler version of 'some guy told me'—that later his bowels were parted from his body. A stone table in St. Paul's commemorating Lancaster became the setting for further supposed miracles, surrounded by weeping, hysterical imbeciles.

In August 1322, Edward invaded Scotland and declared that 'we have found no resistance,' but this was only because the Scots had simply disappeared beyond the River Forth to conduct the usual guerrilla warfare. The English troops retreated with their loot, which in total added up to one lame cow, but the Scots followed them and, on October 22 at Old Byland in Yorkshire, they inflicted a smaller but more humiliating defeat than Bannockburn. The English soldiers ran away and Edward fled to the coast where a boat took him to safety, leaving his jewels and the captured Earl of Richmond.

For a second time, he had left his wife at the mercy of his enemies, for Isabella—in Tynemouth Priory in Northumberland—was cut off by the Scots. Edward sent her letters but made no attempt at rescue, and instead ordered for Despenser's cronies to come. She refused to go, as she didn't trust them, and finally escaped by sea, where two of her ladies died en route, one in labor and another falling overboard.

Edward ruled in a way that didn't exactly command loyalty. In 1323, Andrew Harclay, hero of the battle of Boroughbridge in which Lancaster was defeated, decided that the war could only be ended by negotiating with Robert the Bruce. So he met him. However, when Edward and Despenser learned of this, they had him immediately executed, and it was decreed that Harclay should be drawn, hanged, and beheaded: 'That your heart, and bowels and entrails, whence came your traitorous thoughts, be torn out and burnt to ashes and that the ashes be scattered to winds; that your body be cut into four quarters,' and sent to Carlisle, Newcastle, York, and Shrewsbury, and the head set on London Bridge.

Then, in 1324, the new king of France, Isabella's brother Charles IV, invaded Gascony; the English defenders had to buy a six-month truce and give away a lot of land. This new Anglo-French war was obviously bad for the queen; Despenser had her lands confiscated and her household was purged, with French subjects interned. On top of this, her three children were taken and put into the custody of Despenser's wife and sister.

Isabella was then sent to France in March 1325 on a diplomatic mission to make peace with her brother, along with a relatively small entourage of thirty-one attendants who had been specially chosen for their loyalty to Despenser. Fatefully, there she would meet Roger Mortimer, who had managed to escape from the Tower on August 1, 1323, using the oldest trick in the book (although maybe it wasn't old at the time). It was the feast day of Saint Peter ad Vincula, patron saint of the Tower church, which was always marked by heavy drinking by the guards. Mortimer's friends had turned Gerard de Alspaye, the sublieutenant of the tower, who spiked everyone's drinks including his own (to make it look like he wasn't involved). They hacked into the side of his cell so Mortimer could crawl into the king's kitchen, and then with a rope ladder he escaped up roofs and walls to the river where a boat took him to Hainault across the North Sea.

After Mortimer escaped, Despenser became convinced that his enemy's supporters were using necromancy—black magic—and he wrote to the pope complaining he was threatened by their 'magical and secret dealings.' The pope was not persuaded and replied that no remedies were necessary, only that 'the Holy Father recommends him to turn to God with his whole heart.' Which wasn't likely.

In France, Isabella met her brother Charles who agreed to confirm English possession of Gascony without forcing King Edward to come to Paris to do homage, but instead allowing his eldest son Edward to do so instead. The queen persuaded the king to allow Prince Edward to travel to France to spare him the humiliation of doing so, after which they would both return. He agreed, a fatal error, and after the boy followed his mother in September 1325, the Despensers soon realized they had been outwitted. With the prince in her possession, Isabella was far more dangerous.

King Edward ordered his son and wife to return; otherwise, she would 'feel his wrath all the days of his life.' She said no, Charles refused to expel his sister, and Prince Edward preferred to stay with his mother.

Isabella had complained: 'I feel that marriage is a joining together of man and woman, and someone has come between my husband and myself trying to break this bond. I protest that I will not return until this intruder is removed, but, discarding my marriage garment, [I] shall assume the robes of widowhood and mourning until I am avenged of this Pharisee.' The king, however, seems to have been totally unaware for some time just how much his wife hated him; even in 1321, he ordered special dress-lengths for the queen and her damsel for Christmas, and now that she was in France 'he continued to write to her the puzzled, faintly querulous letters of a kindly husband who cannot imagine what has gone wrong.'[18] What could have upset her?

Roger Mortimer was still in the Flanders at the time and came to France for a funeral where he began a fateful affair with the queen. Roger was a married father of ten, so her family did not entirely approve of the relationship.

Isabella was also joined by King Edward's half brother, the Earl of Kent (who was also Isabella's nephew, confusingly), and leading nobles such as the Earl of Richmond, as well as two senior bishops, who had all turned against the regime. The queen of England was declared an enemy alien and her lands confiscated for the safety of the kingdom, but with a small force she arrived in England in October 1326, along with Mortimer and her son. Edward's other half brother, the Earl of Norfolk, who was in charge of the defense of East Anglia, now went over to Isabella's side.

London's mob showed its support for the invasion the only way it knew how on October 15. That day, Bishop Stapledon, the king's ally, happened to be riding through the city on the way back from a Mass. Walter Stapledon, who was also treasurer, was a man the chronicler *Vita* called 'immeasurably greedy'; he was also one of the first Englishmen to wear glasses, an invention that had just come out of Italy. As agitation against the regime reached fever pitch, the bishop was chased by a mob, and, having tried to get sanctuary at St. Paul's, was dragged off his horse and beheaded with a bread knife. The head was sent to the queen. Meanwhile, Prince Edward was proclaimed 'guardian of the realm' that same month.

Edward and the younger Despenser had tried to flee by boat from Chepstow in Wales, but spent six days at sea, since the wind would not change, and they had to go back, where they were captured. Despenser the Elder had been separated from them days earlier and was caught in Bristol where he was hauled before a tribunal including Mortimer, Lancaster's brother Henry, Kent, and Norfolk. He was obviously not going to be let off, and was dragged through the city streets and hanged from the city gallows. His head was carried on a spear to Winchester; his gruesome punishment seems to have been designed as an ironic parody of Lancaster's. His body was fed to the dogs.

The younger Despenser had tried to starve himself to death while in custody, so they brought the execution forward. Naked but for a crown of nettles and mocking verse carved on his skin with knives, he was dragged through the city of Hereford by four horses to the sound of trumpets and bagpipes, and half hanged on a fifty-foot-tall gallows so that everyone could get a good look. He was stripped and 'hoisted, choking and kicking' by a noose, then the rope was lowered so he could see the executioner's knife coming to castrate him. A fire was lit under the scaffold, and Despenser's genitals were thrown in, followed by his intestines and heart, the dying man watching everything. The crowd cheered as his head was cut off.

In January 1327, Lords and Commons were called in the name of Edward's son, with Mortimer appointed Keeper of the Realm, the first time Parliament effectively chose a king. Mortimer declared that the magnates had deposed Edward because he had not followed his coronation oath and was under the control of evil advisers. The Archbishop of Canterbury concluded that Edward should be deposed because everyone wished it: *vox populi, vox Dei*. In Kenilworth Castle, the king was confronted by his opponents and did not take their advice to abdicate well, 'weeping and fainting.' According to the bishop of Hereford, Edward carried around a knife with which to kill Isabella, and said he'd bite her to death if need be. Clearly the marriage had some problems by this stage.

The king was moved to Berkeley Castle in Gloucestershire, where he was mistreated, mocked, and made to shave off his hair and beard with cold water from a ditch, then dressed in old clothes, with a crown of hay placed on his head, and stuck in a cesspit filled with stinking animal carcasses. It was hoped he'd die of food poisoning, but he proved resilient.

The usurpers moved the king from castle to castle, not knowing what to do with the prisoner, before it was decided that they'd do away with him. Mortimer wanted it to look unsuspicious, so it seems strange that their method of murder was to stick a red-hot poker up his anus. Hardly the most obvious form of suicide anyone would choose.[19]

Although Edward II was a hopeless and tyrannical king, and his wife had every reason to get rid of him, she lost the PR battle. Isabella became known as a *ferrea virago*, a woman who abandoned feminine qualities, or a 'she-wolf,' partly because England would soon become embroiled in a century-long war with her country of birth, but also because she and Mortimer would prove to be just as bad, if not worse, than the regime they replaced.

CHAPTER FIVE

War

The great Italian poet Petrarch wrote toward the end of the century that 'In my youth they [the English] were regarded as the most timid of the uncouth races . . . lower even than the miserable Scots.' In other words, they were barbarians, but not even very effective, scary ones. Compared to Italy, the English certainly were uncouth, but over the next few decades they proved themselves to be anything but timid.

The new king, Edward III, had inherited the strong personalities of his grandfathers, with disastrous consequences for both of their countries. Blessed with the 'face of a god,' according to a contemporary, he was revered by later English rulers as the pinnacle of monarchy and chivalry. The mad King George III, of losing America fame, commissioned Benjamin West to paint scenes of Edward's reign, while Victoria and Albert used to dress up as Edward and his wife Philippa of Hainault. Such was Edward's perceived greatness that even his enemy, France's Charles V, hung a portrait of him in his study.

Edward was the epitome of chivalry and did much to create the pageantry and pomp we associate with England, as well as English national identity, even though it's debatable whether he could even speak English very well and he certainly had to have a tutor.[1] He also brought his country into a brutal, prolonged, and often pointless war, leading thousands of orc-like English criminals across France; funnily enough he was not so appreciated there.

Edward lived for war, was good at it, and clearly enjoyed it. Aged just fifteen, the young king had been put in charge of the English troops on the Scottish border, and at one point he offered to move back a couple of hundred yards from the river so 'that the Scots might have a proper foothold and room to fight.'[2] Things like that gave Edward his reputation for chivalry, although it was also the case that he just loved fighting and would have been disappointed if the Scots had to surrender.

Despite this heroism, Edward comes across as one of the least interesting personalities of the period because he was so lacking in complexity: he loved fighting, women, and sport, and had no major character flaws. He was 'uncomplicated and likeable . . . flamboyant, extrovert, and generous,' loved practical jokes and fancy-dress parties, as well as tournaments, where he fought with the 'same reckless courage that he would later show in battle.'[3] He also had what is now called the common touch, getting on well with the hooligans who constituted most of the English army, playing archery with the foot soldiers, and joking around with his minstrels' kettledrums. Unlike many monarchs of the time, he didn't care about taking revenge and even the sons of enemies could rise up, so that uniquely for this period he had almost 'unconditional political support' among his powerful subjects.[4] But although not begrudging, there was one man he had to remove.

Roger Mortimer had soon made himself hated, and 'lived in a style of pomp and luxury that put the royal court in the shade,' having a Round Table built where jousts and feasts were held.[5] In 1329, he had styled himself as King Arthur at a magnificent tournament with Isabella playing Guinevere; the king's mother, meanwhile, had doubled her already extremely generous annual income. The pair of them quickly wrecked the country's finances, so that crown reserves decreased from over sixty thousand pounds in 1326 to just forty-one pounds in 1330. Mortimer had given himself the grand title Earl of March and became as unpopular as the Despensers, whose lordships he had taken. One historian described him as 'perhaps the nastiest man ever to rule England,' an accolade with some tough competition.[6]

The new regime further lost support by making the realistic but unpopular decision to recognize Scotland's independence. In March 1328, a treaty was signed at Edinburgh in which the English accepted Robert the Bruce as king, with full authority to deal with other heads of state. As part of the deal, Edward's sister Joan was betrothed to Bruce's son David, and young Edward was so angry he didn't attend the marriage ceremony in Berwick, reduced to tears by the 'shameful peace of Northampton.'

Thomas of Lancaster's brother Henry had tried to stay out of politics since inheriting the title, but along with other noblemen he became alarmed at the direction of the government, and, in 1328, he was one of a number to refuse to attend Parliament. In January 1329, Lancaster, along with the king's uncles, the Earls of Kent and Norfolk, marched into London. But Isabella and Mortimer's army attacked their territories in the midlands, and so Lancaster surrendered.

Edmund of Kent was soon arrested on suspicion of treason and then entrapped in a way a Victorian might call 'unsporting.' Mortimer had hired two *agent provocateurs*, Dominican friars, to trick his prisoner into believing his brother Edward II was still alive and was ready to return. There was a rumor that Edward had survived to become a wandering hermit in Cologne, a quite common myth attached to dead medieval kings; Harold II was thought by some to have survived the Battle of Hastings to live as a hermit, while the German Emperor Heinrich V is supposed to have ended up in Cheshire.

Sick of the new regime, Kent fell for the ruse by pledging his support to the former king, and was quickly sentenced to death. On the day of his execution he was led out of Winchester Castle, but he had to wait five hours on the scaffold as no one could be found to behead him until eventually a felon agreed to do the job in exchange for his own death sentence being postponed. When Edmund's head was raised, the crowd remained silent.

The young king, installed as a puppet, could trust so few people that he smuggled a letter to the pope saying only notes with the words *pater sancte*, 'holy father,' could be treated as genuine; otherwise, it could be Mortimer's handiwork. In 1330, he decided to act and, aged just seventeen, led a small band of friends his own age in a *Goonies*-like action-adventure, capturing Mortimer at Nottingham Castle (admittedly an especially violent remake of the *Goonies*). The suspicious Mortimer had every gate and door locked and barred, while the queen looked after the keys and forbade her son from entering, but Edward had told the constable of the castle to leave a door unlocked, and that night he entered the fortress with twenty-five young men. After the teenagers killed three courtiers, Mortimer was captured standing behind a curtain trying to put his armor on.

The queen begged her son to 'spare gentle Mortimer,' but the man responsible for the death of Edward's father was now tried at Westminster while forced to wear a cloak with the phrase *quid gloriaris* emblazed on it—'where's your glory now?' Inevitably, he was sentenced to hang, though spared disembowelment as a concession to Isabella, and his body left to rot for two days at Tyburn. The Tyburn tree, west of London, had been a popular execution spot since 1196 when the populist irritant William Fitzosbert had been hanged, and it remained a place of execution for several centuries, popularly known as 'God's tribunal.' So popular were hangings there that locals would put up temporary stands and charge people to watch, although on one occasion these collapsed, causing dozens of fatalities. The last Tyburn hanging took place in 1763, by which time residents in the increasingly fashionable West End district thought the site of rotting corpses might be lowering the tone of the area a little bit. The spot where the tree stood is now Marble Arch, London's rather feeble imitation of the Arc de Triomphe.[7]

Edward's mother, meanwhile, managed to get off pretty lightly; she was banished to an enormous country estate in Norfolk where her son continued to send her gifts of boar, lovebirds, and wine. She continued to enjoy four thousand pounds a year in allowances and regularly traveled to the capital, where she liked to borrow romance stories from the Tower of London's library. Strangely, at court, Edward would dress as Sir Lancelot and his mother as Lancelot's lover Guinevere, the queen in silk and silver garnished with six hundred rubies and eighteen hundred pearls, and 'attended by minstrels, huntsmen, and grooms.'[8] She died in 1358 and was buried in her wedding gown next to the heart of the husband she utterly despised.

Edward, meanwhile, had enjoyed his first military victory on the boggy ground of Halidon Hill in 1333 against a force of Scots twice as large—the start of a long glorious reign of violence.

116 Years' War

The Victorians called it the Hundred Years' War, although it lasted 116 years and was more like three wars with long intervals in between.[9] The conflict would later become about Edward III's claim to the throne of France through his mother, but it was really about wine, or at least the region where England got its supply: the Duchy of Gascony. The French crown claimed the province, which was still subject to the King of England, and the only way Edward could fight them without losing the support of the pope was to declare himself king of France.

Later, it would turn into a war of naked aggression by the English, without the slightest pretense of any reason except theft. For the ordinary people in regions such as Normandy it was fantastically grim, as their country was overrun by the dregs of England and mercenaries from across Europe, and eventually even Edward lost control of the bands of delinquents running around France. Ultimately, though, the war would not just bankrupt the English crown, but would also lead to what intelligence officials these days call 'blow back'—a civil war back home.

Gascony, the area south of Bordeaux, was ruled by the king of England, although only as a vassal of the king of France, part of the complex system of feudalism that kept the peace but often left some curious anomalies; the French monarch was overlord to most of the regions we now call France even if he sometimes only ruled a small chunk around Paris and much of the rest was in reality independent. Below him were the twelve peers of France—effective rulers in some cases—among them Edward in his role as Duke of Guyenne (another name for Aquitaine, of which Gascony formed the southern part)[10] and Count of Ponthieu.

Bordeaux, a city of thirty thousand people, owed its wealth to wine exports, in particular to the English who drank 'several times more claret per head than they do today.'[11] Wine buffs tend to consider Bordeaux to be the best wine region in the world, and its vintages can sell for vast amounts of money, so it is hardly surprising that the English were keen to keep hold of it. Because of its wine, the region brought in more money for the crown than the whole of England.

The economies of the two countries were closely interlinked, so that the Gascon Henri le Waleys was mayor of both Bordeaux and London. Many Gascons worked in England, often in the army, and took an active part in the wars against the Scots. The Plantagenet monarchs, said one historian, 'regarded Guyenne as a far more integral part of their domains than Wales or Ireland, and Froissart often refers to Guyennois as "the English."'[12] They also regarded the northern French as a separate people, and even as late as the 1789 Revolution referred to those from the North as 'Franchiman' and themselves as 'Romans,' reflecting the fact that northern France had been settled by Germanic Franks while those in the South were more Latin.[13] And with only two hundred English officials in the region, the Gascons were mostly left to run their own affairs, which is why they preferred to be ruled by London rather than Paris.[14]

At the time, France had a population of twenty-one million, compared to just four or five million in England, but France was hopelessly divided and had no real cohesion. Even in the nineteenth century, most people in the country could not speak 'French,' with regional identity being far stronger; England, in contrast, was quite small and homogenous, with the exception of the very far north.

The mirror image of Gascony was Scotland, which the kings of England saw themselves as overlords of, but which the Scots viewed rather differently. Naturally, they formed an 'auld alliance' with France.

The death of Philippe's last son Charles IV in 1328 led to a succession crisis. He left only a pregnant wife and if she produced a son, he would become king; otherwise, the crown would be up in the air with the most likely candidate being a cousin called Philippe of Valois. On April Fool's Day, the widowed queen gave birth to a daughter, so she was forgotten about; Valois got the assembly in Paris to proclaim him Philippe VI.

Both the new kings of France and England were aggressive, alpha-male types—Philippe was a champion jouster—so they were inevitably going to end up fighting, and relations soured fairly quickly. As a prince, Edward had already done homage to the French for Gascony, but, in 1329, Philippe invited him to Amiens to do so again. The Frenchman was furious when his opposite number turned up in a crimson velvet robe with golden leopard prints, sporting a crown on his head along with spurs and a sword. He was supposed to arrive bareheaded, but refused when his overlord demanded it; it was on the basis of such things that wars were started.

The encounter was complicated by numerous conflicts within France, and was stirred up by a succession of embittered aristocrats who arrived at Edward's court encouraging the not-super-bright king to invade. The first of these was Robert of Artois, a leading

French nobleman of dubious virtue, who had fled to England after poisoning his aunt to claim her inheritance for which he was sentenced to death. Robert was described as 'a violent and dishonest adventurer with many enemies' but also 'flamboyant and charming, an excellent horseman and a skillful flatterer, in fact just the kind of man that Edward liked.'[15] Philippe had said anyone who harbored Robert was an enemy, so Edward gave him three castles and made him an earl. In December 1336, the French demanded Robert's extradition, and the following May Philippe VI finally attacked Gascony, so starting the Hundred Years' War effectively.

As Duke of Gascony, Edward could not declare war on his feudal overlord because the pope would excommunicate him. He soon concluded that the only way he could actually take hold of the region was to claim the throne of France itself. By most succession rules Edward had a better case than Philippe, through his mother, but queens could not rule because, as the contemporary historian Froissant said, 'the realm of France was so noble it must not fall into a woman's hands,' and so the French then rationalized that the throne could not even pass through the female line. This Salic Law, supposedly the ancient rule of the Franks, was only made up later. The real reason Edward could not become king was that he was a foreign ruler and Philippe already had a large power base in the country.

It was Robert of Artois who managed to convince Edward to start the war, according to one famous story, by presenting him with a heron at a feast—a deliberate insult since it was considered the coward of the bird world. Edward's response was to swear an oath to 'cross the sea, my subjects with me . . . set the country ablaze and . . . await my mortal enemy, Philippe of Valois, who wears the fleur-delis . . . I renounce him, you can be sure of that, for I will make war on him by word and deed.' This story was satirical, designed to make Edward look idiotic, but he did seem to be easily swayed.

To make matters more complicated, the war also involved Flanders, in what is now Belgium, a very rich country that was theoretically subject to the king of France but was in practice independent with extensive trading links with England. Flanders was divided between its pro-English and pro-French elements, and, in 1338, the pro-English Jacob van Artevelde became 'Hooftman' of Ghent and, after taking most of Flanders, 'put to death anyone who opposed him.' It was his Flemish allies who persuaded Edward to claim the throne because only then could they justify their own behavior by saying they were just doing their duty as vassals of the king of France. Even Edward didn't take the claim seriously, yet he could never drop it without admitting the war was unjust, and so it developed a life of its own. For various reasons, the English didn't officially drop the claim until 1802, by which time there was no king of France anymore, as the last one had his head chopped off in front of a baying mob.

In August 1337, Edward also made a pact with his wife's brother-in-law, the Holy Roman Emperor Ludwig IV, who, despite his title, had been excommunicated by the pope. The emperor, who theoretically ruled most of what is now Germany, although very loosely and vaguely had promised him help against Philippe for seven years and offered to make Edward vicar-general (or deputy) of the Empire. However, Edward had to bribe the Germans to join with £120,000 in payments, and so when he raised an army in 1337, the cost was already a staggering two hundred thousand pounds, several times his annual income.

In 1338, the French sacked Southampton; that year, Guernsey in the Channel Islands was also occupied, and the following year, the French raided the coast from Cornwall to Kent, attacking Dover and Folkestone and burning down much of the Isle of Wight. On March 23, 1339, Philippe had even issued an *ordonnance*—battle plan—for the full conquest of England, although he never carried it out. It was partly because of this terror and hatred of the French that the conflict was popular in England, and Edward was able to gather the support of the aristocracy, in particular the group of one hundred barons, bishops, and abbots who really mattered.[16] There was also a great deal of enthusiasm for invading France because, unlike Scotland, there was huge opportunity for theft.

Although most of the English warlords were from the landed aristocracy, there were scores of 'needy adventurers of obscure birth and no inherited property [who] made notable fortunes.'[17] The war offered many humble-born men the chance to come up in the world, most of them awful human beings and by today's standards war criminals. There was Sir John Chandos, a poor knight from Derbyshire, and Sir Thomas Dagworth, 'a bold professional soldier' who came from a middle-class Norfolk family, both of whom rose from obscurity to play a leading part in the war before dying horrifically violent deaths. John Hawkwood, the leader of the largest and most dangerous mercenary army, was the son of an Essex tanner.[18]

Edward's army was drawn from a 'commissions of array' and the commissioners—usually locals with military experience—were given the job of choosing men from their area to fight. Naturally the commissioners mostly picked the dregs of society who served no useful purpose back home, and it is estimated that 12 percent of Edward's army were outlaws, most of those murderers who could obtain a 'charter of pardon' if they fought. Many of the notorious gang members of the 1320s and 1330s ended up being pardoned and some even got knighthoods.

However, while he was in the Low Countries, Edward's supply of money dried up, which was not a good start. He blamed the lack of cash reaching him in Antwerp on treachery, and tried to stop the salaries of all officials and ministers until he was persuaded they would all resign if he did this. The problem was that the king had 'little understanding of the problems of taxation or credit and was bored by administration' and all his invasions were done on 'a hand-to-mouth basis, without budgets or forecasts.'[19] He just didn't understand that you couldn't fund wars in three different places at the same time, and despite Parliament voting in new taxes, Edward was already so broke that he left his pregnant wife Philippa in Ghent as security, as he could not pay the Flemish the money he promised them; while there, his wife gave birth to a son who therefore became known as John of Gaunt. The king told Parliament in the spring of 1340 that unless they raised more taxes he would be imprisoned for debt by the Flemish, which would probably be a bit humiliating.

In September 1339, Edward arrived in France with fifteen thousand men, including many German and Dutch mercenaries who were notorious at the time. Philippe, despite having thirty-five thousand men, didn't show up, leaving Edward with troops threatening to go home. This was the favored French tactic since they guessed the English would run out of money and food and become restless and leave. Edward, meanwhile, sent insulting letters to Philippe offering one-on-one combat, which the forty-seven-year-old was hardly likely to accept from a man twenty years younger, or alternatively to combat between one hundred of the best knights selected by each. The Frenchman did not take up his offer.

The first battle of the war took place in Sluys in Flanders, where the English defeated a navy twice as large and left so many of their enemy dead that it was said that if fish spoke, they could have learned French.

Sluys was a textbook case of French bureaucratic inflexibility. Their navy was led by a Genoese sailor with the suitably terrifying name Barbanera, or Blackbeard, and included Genoese war galleys with rams and catapults, but despite their advantage the French were, characteristically, hamstrung by a horror of anything that contradicted correct procedure in that charming way the French have. So Blackbeard had to ask permission of the two French leaders in charge, Hugues Quieret and Nicolas Behuchet, before doing anything despite the fact they weren't even sailors—Behuchet was a tax collector. So they stayed in anchor and when Edward arrived, the more powerful French ships were trapped.

In the course of the day, the English destroyed or captured 190 of 213 French boats, and some sixteen to eighteen thousand French soldiers and seamen died, as well as all of Philippe's admirals. A chronicler recorded: 'The sea was so full of corpses that those who did not drown could not tell whether they were swimming in water or blood, though the knights must have gone straight to the bottom in their heavy armor.' Blackbeard, seeing what a disaster it was, led his men away. The two French leaders surrendered, but Quieret was immediately beheaded and Buhechet was hanged after a few minutes and left on the galley to demoralize the French.

All throughout, Edward was in the thick of the fighting, getting blood splattered on his white leather boots. The battle ended with thirty French ships fleeing, with only one ship—the *Saint-Jacques of Dieppe*—continuing to fight into the night; when it was finally captured by the Earl of Huntingdon, four hundred corpses were found on board the ship.

The worst tragedy for the English occurred when one of their ships was sunk carrying 'a great number of countesses, ladies, knights' wives, and other damsels, that were going to see the Queen at Ghent' after being struck by cannon. Bizarrely, wives were quite often brought along to watch battles, 'health and safety' not really being a thing at the time.

Edward commemorated the victory by making a special gold coin worth six shillings and eight pence, which showed him on board a ship on the waves with a crown on his head and carrying an impressive sword and shield. This sort of propaganda went down very well at home, where there wasn't much reflection on the pity and horror of war.[20]

Afterward, no one wanted to tell King Philippe about the disaster so it was left to a jester.

'Our knights are far braver than the English,' he said.

'Why is that?' the king asked.

'Because the English don't dare to jump into the sea in full armor.'

However, despite this glorious victory, two years later the French were able to sack Plymouth again, and Edward soon had to give up in France as he was running out of money. He came back furious and convinced that it was all the fault of his ministers for not finding him enough money, blaming the chancellor and archbishop of Canterbury, John Stratford. Edward, bizarrely, told the pope that Stratford had deliberately kept the king short of money in the hope that he would be killed because he wanted to have sex with the queen. Stratford had to take sanctuary in Canterbury, terrified the monarch would have him executed.

In 1341, Edward was so broke that he couldn't repay his loans, including £180,000 borrowed from Florentine bankers. Because of him, in 1343, the Peruzzi family went bankrupt, still owing seventy-seven thousand pounds even before interest; the following year another powerful banking family, the Bardi, also went under.

However, soon another angry aristocrat turned up in England, a Norman knight called Geoffrey d'Harcourt who wanted the English to invade because the French king had given his beloved, one Jeanne Bacon, to a crony to marry. The knight, 'another volatile adventurer, a man of hopeless dreams rather like Robert of Artois,'[21] told Edward to come to Normandy because there was 'so much booty' and 'no one would resist.'

Edward couldn't refuse such a suggestion and he sailed for Normandy in June 1346 with fifteen thousand men including many of the usual riffraff. They arrived in Caen and when the people in the city saw the army approaching they fled in horror, falling over one another in their rush to escape. Which was wise, as after some of the locals had thrown rocks and metal from the rooftops at the invaders, Edward ordered for the entire town to be slaughtered and burnt; although d'Harcourt persuaded him that this might be a bit excessive, some three thousand were killed.

A new word entered the English language around this time, originally from Italian—*plunder*. After Caen was ransacked, the king 'sent into England his navy of ships charged with clothes, jewels, vessels of gold and silver, and other riches, and of prisoners more than 60 knights and 300 burgesses,' who would be ransomed. A chronicler called Thomas Walsingham wrote in 1348: 'there were few women who did not possess something from Caen, Calais or another town over the seas, such as clothing, furs and cushions. Tablecloths and linen were seen in everybody's houses. Married women were decked in the trimmings of French matrons and if the latter bemoaned their loss the former exulted in their gain.'

Unfortunately for the French, while in Caen, Edward found documentary proof of Philippe's 1339 *ordonnance*, and this made him even angrier. He ordered for copies to be made and read in every parish in England, including by the archbishop of Canterbury at St. Paul's so 'that he might thereby rouse the people.' To further his propaganda war, he also employed Dominican friars to go around from town to town explaining why the war was happening, a sort of fourteenth-century version of 'Why We Fight.' (The short answer: to steal tablecloths.)

Meanwhile, the Flemish poet Froissart became the king's chronicler; born in Hainault in 1337, he was described as 'the first war correspondent,' but he painted the king in a flattering manner.

After destroying Caen, the English headed in the direction of Paris, using the favorite tactic of the *chevauchée*, 'a rather glamorous term for what was essentially a traveling riot of looting, burning, rape, and murder.'[22] Its original meaning was a sort of horse ride or jaunt, but it came to mean going through an area and burning, stealing, and killing everything and everyone in sight, thereby forcing the local lord to fight. Edward wrote a letter to his eldest son, Edward the Black Prince, saying 'our people are burning and destroying to the breadth and depth 12 or 14 leagues of the country' and 'so that the country is quite laid waste of corn, of cattle and of any other goods.' He meant it as a good thing, like a progress report, rather than a lament about the woe of war—he also mentioned that the city of Cambrai in Flanders had been 'laid waste.' Good-o. (He did have some limits, however, and ordered that no church be attacked, hanging twenty of his men who had set fire to one in Beauvais.)

One English knight, Sir Geoffrey Scrope, took a French cardinal 'up a great and high tower, showing him the whole countryside towards Paris for a distance of fifteen miles burning in every place.'[23] He asked him, 'Sir, does it not seem to you that the silken thread encompassing France is broken?' and the cardinal collapsed. A yes, in other words.

After Caen, Edward's army of eight thousand men, half of them archers, marched through Normandy on their way to Paris. North of the capital they turned around to join their Flemish allies, and the French king trudged across the River Somme to catch them. The two sides met on August 13, 1346, at a place called Crecy-en-Ponthieu, where probably the greatest victory in English history was won.

CHAPTER SIX

Crecy

H alf a century earlier, when the English had defeated the Welsh, they were so impressed with their enemies that they drafted them into their army. Even more than the soldiers, however, they were amazed with a Welsh invention, the longbow, which had a devastating effect on the French cavalry.

At the time, the most advanced weapon was the crossbow, which was considered so frightening when it was first introduced in the twelfth century that the Church tried banning its use. However, the new weapon, despite looking more primitive, could fire off up to twelve iron-tipped arrows a minute, compared to the crossbow's four, and its arrows were lethal at a range of 150 yards (while at sixty yards they could pierce plate armor). In the first minute at Crecy, the Anglo-Welsh archers fired seventy thousand arrows, each archer letting off his sixth missile before the first one had landed.

It took years of experience to get good at the longbow, which usually lead to chronic spine problems, and since Edward I's reign, such practice had been mandatory with 'every yokel being commanded by law to practice at the butts on Sunday.' Longshanks also banned football, as it distracted from archery, although the street violence associated with the sport also unnerved the authorities. The two constants of English life through the centuries are (1) heavy alcohol use, and (2) an inability to see a soccer ball without having a mass brawl, usually also involving constant (1). In France, meanwhile, owning a weapon was banned because it made the aristocracy nervous and, however much the English frightened them, they feared and despised their own peasants more.

A further act of 1369 also banned hockey, handball, cockfighting, and 'other such idle games' on pain of imprisonment, while another law decreed that if an archer killed a man while practicing then it should not be considered a crime. Up and down the country, young men larked about with arrows tipped with sharp steel that were able to penetrate an oak door four inches thick, at a time when the average person consumed eight pints of beer a day. What could go wrong?

Archers were well paid, especially mounted archers who got six pence a day, which was the same as a master craftsman; the foot archer received three pence, which compared well to a good plowman who made two pence. Mounted archers on ponies—who did not actually fire while mounted—were first used by Edward III in Scotland; a group from Cheshire would form a two hundred-strong royal bodyguard, all dressed in green and white uniforms. By 1346, the longbow was standardized with each archer carrying two-dozen arrows, backed by further supplies.

The longbow did much to undermine the class system because archers were so effective against mounted knights, who, because of the costs involved, had always been exclusively upper class. In the fourteenth century, plate armor—the full coats of armor that traditionally feature as comic props in stately homes in cartoons— replaced chain mail, which was of no use against direct sword attacks. The new material was incredibly heavy, dark, and stuffy inside, 'a terrible worm in an iron cocoon' as one former soldier described it, and men would often have heart attacks just walking around in the thing. It was also expensive, although horses were the biggest cost. The term 'man-at-arms' applied to those classes—knight-bannerets, knight-bachelors, and esquires—who could afford two armed valets and three mounts per men-at-arms, a warhorse, a packhorse for armor, and a palfrey (a cheap horse) to ride outside of battle. All of this required a fair bit of money as the giant warhorses of this period cost the huge sum of two hundred pounds (for that you could get a horse trained to bite opponents).

The war also saw the first use of firearms, although it was not until the very end of the conflict that they became hugely effective. In 1345, Edward ordered the making of one hundred ribaults, which fired twelve metal balls at high speed, but 'such weapons were seldom lethal, except to those firing them' although 'they produced plenty of noise, flame, and acrid black smoke.'[1]

The main weapon of both the French and English soldiers was a dagger called a *misericord* or mercy-killer, so-called as it usually finished off the fatally wounded; soldiers wore the dagger on the right with a long sword on their left, although the Welsh footmen wore long knives on the back of their belts, which some historians think added to the long-established myth that Englishmen had tails.

At Crecy, the French heavily outnumbered the English with fifteen thousand Genoese crossbowmen, twenty thousand men at arms, thousands of knights on horseback, and a lot more peasants. As well as their four thousand archers, the English had just two thousand foot soldiers and fifteen hundred knifemen. However, the French troops did not reach the battlefield until 4 p.m. when the sun was in their eyes; they were also tired after a long march, and their bowstrings were wet from a storm, while the English and Welsh had protected theirs by rolling them in their helmets. Had the French waited until morning they would probably have won.

Worried there would be a scramble to capture high-value opponents, at the start of the battle the French unfurled the *oriflamme* flag, signifying that there would be no prisoners. The king of England followed suit.

However, with a hail of English arrows the Genoese crossbowmen soon ran off, and after three courageous assaults, the French were caught in the mud, helpless as the arrows rained down. Afterward, Welsh knifemen were sent in after dark to sneak under the enemies' horses and cut open their stomachs, and then the Frenchmen above them.

Although King Edward was still barely in his midthirties, at an age many men today are still basically adolescents, alongside him in battle was his son Edward of Woodstock, known to history as the Black Prince because of his distinctive armor, who was aged just sixteen.[2] During the fight, he was knocked off his feet and left helpless in his mail, at which point the standard bearer Richard de Beaumont covered him with the banner of Wales and heroically protected him from being killed until he was able to get up. Although Froissart has a story about Edward refusing to help his son with the quote, 'Let the boy win his spurs for I want him, please God to have all the glory,' another contemporary, Geoffrey le Baker, says the king sent twenty knights to relieve his son—which seems more likely.

By the end of the day, fifteen hundred French noblemen and ten thousand of their regular soldiers lay dead. Among the fallen was fifty-year-old King John of faraway Bohemia, who wanted to get involved in the fighting despite being totally blind. Twelve of his best men chose to tie all their horses together so they could lead their king into battle and, rather unsurprisingly, all but two were killed—'found the next day lying around their leader with their horses still fastened together.'

King John, who had lost his eyesight while on Crusade in Lithuania, was one of the more colorful figures in the war. In the words of one writer, he 'loved fighting for its own sake, not caring whether the conflict was important,' and in between wars he would enter tournaments.[3] Although most likely it was because of an infection, his subjects believed he was struck blind after digging up the tomb of Saint Adelbert in Prague Cathedral to get at money hidden there.

According to popular legend, so impressed was the Black Prince by this noble act of heroic stupidity that he took John's emblem of three ostrich feathers and the motto *Ich Dien*, German for 'I serve,' as his own, and today it is still the emblem of the Prince of Wales. Unfortunately, there's no evidence it's actually true.

Although the rain and sun didn't help, the French also lost because they were too busy showing off, as the whole aim of chivalry was to be at the center of the glory; little thought was given to actual tactics, and chaotic groups of horsemen were vulnerable to well-organized archers. The chivalric ideal was all about being flashy, such Victorian ideas as modesty and reticence being unknown, and even fashion reflected this; knights at this time wore *poulaines*, excessively long, pointed shoes that had to be tied up around the calf just so the person could walk, while Chaucer criticized the wearing of codpieces over trousers and the flaunting of 'shameful privee membres' by men that make it appear like they're suffering a hernia.

Philippe, whose brother Charles was among those killed, fled the scene at the end of the day and found a house where he asked the man to open up to 'the unfortunate king of France,' a pun on his nickname 'the fortunate.'

Crecy also saw the first use of cannon and gunpowder in Europe, which the French had acquired from Italy; originally used by the Chinese in the eighth century, this would change medieval Europe and its feudal system based around castles, impenetrable fortresses that could withstand rebellions or invading armies, but were useless against the new technology.

Around the same time, the English also won a victory over the Scots at Neville's Cross in Durham after King David II made the mistake of invading, which led to inevitable defeat. The king spent nine years in the Tower of London and, to make matters worse, the English also took back 'the Black Rood of Scotland,' supposedly a piece of Christ's Cross kept in a black case. The man who captured

King David, John de Coupland, received five hundred pounds a year for life, but was later murdered by jealous neighbors.

Edward still couldn't conquer Paris, so he marched around it and instead arrived at Calais, which the French had used as a base for raids on English wool ships, and besieged it with thirty thousand men. After the city was reduced to starvation, eventually five hundred of the weakest were sent out, but Edward refused to let them through the lines, and they were left to die. He then demanded everyone surrender, while Philippe withdrew and left the city to its fate; as his troops marched off, the people inside tore down the French coat of arms and threw it over the walls in disgust.

When a leading citizen said he was ready to surrender, Edward replied that the people would be ransomed or killed as in battle, but an English knight persuaded the king to execute just half a dozen leading citizens, sparing the rest. Six men volunteered, walking out of the city stripped to the waist with nooses around their necks. It was all very dramatic and eventually Edward was begrudgingly persuaded by his wife to spare them, allowing the six men to live 'with evident ill-grace.'[4] Queen Phillipa pleading with Edward for the burghers of Calais became a famous theme and was depicted first in a painting by Benjamin West and then on a Rodin sculpture in the city itself, with twelve copies of the sculpture at various spots around the world, including Westminster (by French law no more than twelve replicas can be made, because rules).[5]

After Edward took Calais, he gave each inhabitant a meal before expelling them, and set up an English colony there, part of the general policy that would be called ethnic cleansing today; Calais remained a rather strange outpost of England for another two hundred years, a huge drain on the treasury that the English insisted on keeping.

And the English almost lost the city straightaway. They put an Italian adventurer in charge and, in December 1349, the French bribed the new governor to open the gates to them—and if you can't trust an Italian adventurer who can you trust? Unfortunately, he double-crossed them, the gate was opened, the French leaders walked in, and then the gate shut behind them. On New Year's Eve, they were entertained to dinner by the king of England himself, 'bareheaded save for a chaplet of fine pearls.'

The Order of the Garter

After Calais, Edward went on a victory tour, starring in tournaments and taking in the adulation of the public. The king loved such show business events, which were also a good excuse to dress up; the previous year he had donned an 'exotic green animal outfit for both a joust in which he took part and for that year's Christmas festival at court.'[6]

In honor of his great victory, the king created an order of chivalry on April 23, 1348—St. George's Day. According to one theory, the Order of the Garter had begun as an in-joke between Edward and some of his oldest, most trusted friends, and the use of a garter may have been a bit of lighthearted sexist locker-room humor referencing their wild and carefree younger days. They were in their midthirties, so perhaps the order was the first manifestation of a midlife crisis; nowadays, they'd have just bought Porsches. It was also influenced by the Arthurian legend, which was now reaching its peak, the twenty-four knights of the Garter making up Edward's own Round Table.

It supposedly started in Eltham Palace in Kent, where the king was dancing or in some way was involved in a racy incident with Joan, Countess of Salisbury, said to be the greatest beauty of her age. They were probably lovers, although she was also his future daughter-in-law and ironically known as 'the maiden of Kent' because she was 'the most amorous' of women.

While dancing, the countess's garter slipped from her leg, revealing her stockings, and the room full of men erupted into sniggers. Edward picked up the lady's clothing and tied it around his own leg, exclaiming *Honisoit qui mal y pense* ('Shame on him who thinks evil of it'). Today, it is still the motto of the order, and appears on the masthead of royal crests, as well as in involved *The Times* of London newspaper.

Edward certainly had what used to be called an eye for the ladies, but despite this he had a successful marriage to Philippa of Hainault, with whom he had five sons and three daughters who grew to adulthood. Edward even let his eldest son choose his own wife, extremely unusual at the time, and the other children helped to seal alliances with leading baronial families. This may, however, have helped to ensure future conflict likely because so many leading clans had some claim to the throne.

In practical terms, the Order of the Garter was used as a form of meritocracy. Men who were not part of the actual elite were raised up so that they could be made useful without giving them lands or titles; one of Edward's first nominations was Roger Mortimer, grandson of the man he had killed at Tyburn, who had his land and honor restored after fighting at Crecy. (Of the original twenty-four Order of the Garter members, twenty had been at the battle and two others may have been, including the wonderfully named Sachet d'Abrichecourt.)

The order might have been the idea of Edward's cousin, Henry of Grosmont, Duke of Lancaster and nephew of his father's arch-nemesis. He was known as the 'Father of Soldiers' because he did not miss a battle in forty-five years; even when England was not at war, Lancaster had traveled around Europe looking for conflicts, fighting for Alfonso of Castile against the Moors at the siege of Algeciras in 1343, and in Prussia for the Teutonic Knights in their own Crusade against pagans. While in Spain, Henry would have seen the Order of the Band, Castile's brotherhood of knights, and taken the idea back. Afterward, King Jean of France was so impressed with the Garter that he began his own, the Order of the Star.

In 1352, after returning from Prussia, Lancaster challenged Duke Otto of Brunswick to combat and rode into court in Paris on horseback where he was given an enthusiastic welcome by French nobles, who, despite there being a war and everything, loved a bit of flamboyance. His opponent 'trembled so violently on his war-horse that he could not put on his helmet or wield his spear and had to be removed by his friends and retract his challenge.'[7] Afterward, Lancaster was offered a grand prize as his reward but accepted only a thorn from the 'saviour's crown,' a relic owned by the French king, which he returned home to put in his church in Leicester.[8]

Such was Lancaster's renown in battle that he had been promoted to duke in 1351, and went on to use all his plunder from France to build the Savoy Palace on the Strand, now the site of the famous hotel of the same name.

Chivalric fighting was so popular that there were sometimes tourneys between opposing sides during wars, which happened at Alnwick in 1327 between the English and Scots. During the Crecy campaign, a French knight challenged any comer to three jousts 'for the love of his lady.' An Englishman, Sir Thomas Colville, stepped forward; they fought two but a third fight had to be abandoned.

The same year as the Garter was founded, the king also adopted Saint George as the patron of England, capping off a remarkable rise to power for a saint who was not only foreign but also very obscure. According to tradition, he had been a Roman soldier martyred in the fourth century during the Diocletian persecution, possibly in Libya or Palestine, although the Catholic Church teaches that his acts are 'known only to God.'[9] During the Crusades, western soldiers adopted Saint George after he appeared to them at the siege of Antioch in 1098, and English troops began to ride with his red and white cross into battle.

As the cult became more popular, the method of George's tortured martyrdom became wildly inflated; originally impaled with nails, the story grew so that he was first broken on the wheel, then roasted, boiled and/or burned to death, beheaded, and crucified on a variety of differently shaped crosses, so that at one point the story went that he was brought back to life just so he could be tortured to death again. By another account, he was supposed to have spent seven years dying painfully during a quite fantastically heroic martyrdom. George also went through a process of Anglicization, so by the fourteenth century it was claimed he came from Coventry in the west midlands.

April 23 became a major day in the English calendar from the fourteenth to the seventeenth century, when the Reformation made such religious festivals unpopular; it then came back into fashion after the 1996 European soccer championship, and these days it is mostly marked by torturous newspaper think pieces about the meaning of English national identity. George is also patron saint of Germany, Hungary, Lithuania, Armenia, Ethiopia, Catalonia, farmers, butchers, skin diseases, and the Plague. Meanwhile, native saints such as Edward the Confessor, Alban, and Edmund all declined in importance, and the last two had to make do with having commuter towns named in their honor.

Knighthood wasn't all glamor, however, and knights were already evolving into a sort of modern middle class, the kind of people who do worthy public sector jobs. By the 1220s, county knights were appointed alongside professional lawyers as justices in charge of delivering people to jail, and, in Edward III's reign, many knights were becoming justices of the peace, local magistrates who these days have to deal with juvenile delinquents and suchlike. JPs were ordered to meet regularly in 'quarter sessions,' a system that lasted until the 1970s, and became the basis of local administration and justice, as the role of the upper-middle class evolved from being warrior to lawyer. Today, the Order of the Garter still consists of the monarch and twenty-four knights, and meets every third week of June for a suitably Ruritanian ceremony where they all dress up in quaint outfits, but it has a less military flavor; David Brewer, a former insurance broker, became its 1,008th member in 2016.

CHAPTER SEVEN

Plague

Gunpowder, first used in Crecy, had come by way of Italy, which was far more advanced than France or England both in terms of technology and culture, already showing the signs of the cultural explosion of the following century. In 1305, Giotto had painted the Scrovegni chapel in Padua; Dante, living in Florence, had completed his *Divine Comedy* in 1320; while, in 1345, the first humanist, Petrarch, had discovered Cicero's letters, an event often credited with kick-starting the fifteenth-century Renaissance.

Although Florence was the center of this flowering of culture, Italy's most powerful city-states were Venice and Genoa, whose wealth was built on trade with the East. Among Genoa's numerous trading colonies was Caffa in the Black Sea, which, in 1346, was under assault by the Tartars, a steppes people from central Asia who had once terrorized Eastern Europe.[1]

During the siege of Caffa, the Tartar soldiers began coming down with a mysterious disease that caused them to cough up blood, grow repulsive boils on their groins, and die in agony. The illness soon killed huge numbers of Crimean Tartars, an improbably large figure of eighty-five thousand often given. 'Fatigued, stupefied, and amazed' by this new illness,[2] the Tartars called off the siege, but in an attempt to demoralize their enemies catapulted the dead bodies of the victims over the walls, unaware they had pioneered an early form of biological warfare. The Genoese chucked the corpses in the sea, but it was too late, and soon they were faced with an epidemic. Realizing they could not survive future Tartar attacks in such a weakened state, they traveled in their boats back to Italy. Which the people back home must have really appreciated.

When Christians first heard stories of a new deadly disease that afflicted the Middle East, they thought it was divine retribution against the Turks and Saracens for taking Christian land. This confidence in heavenly support didn't last long, however, and a year after the Caffa siege, Italians in London first heard rumors of people back home dropping dead in huge numbers. Plagues of one sort or another have been a feature of human existence since the first cities were built, and there had been seventy major epidemics in the previous seven centuries. Further back there was the plague of Athens in the fifth century BC and the Justinian Plague that hit after the fall of the Roman Empire. But this new disease, known later as the Black Death, would be worse than anything before or since.

Yersinia pestis, the bacterium that carried the bubonic plague, had been living on gerbils in Tibet for a while and was harmless to other species, but unstable climate conditions in the 1340s caused the disease to mutate. In its new deadly form, it first hit China, which had in the previous years already suffered a series of unimaginable disasters. There had been drought and famine in the Yangtze River region, and a huge earthquake in Ki-Ming-Chan, after which whole mountains collapsed creating a huge lake. Then in Tche province, some five million are said to have died from earthquakes and floods from 1337–1345. There was also the Mongol invasion.

Not that Europe was having a great time either, for even before the Plague arrived, Italy had endured a series of tragedies, so that even without the Plague it would have been an exceptionally awful period. During those grim times, there were earthquakes in Naples,

Rome, Pisa, Bologna, Padua, and Venice; in July 1345, there was six months of rain that ruined crops followed by famine in 1346 and 1347. On top of this, there were a series of banking collapses, workers' riots in many cities, and also a terrible earthquake in January 1348 that destroyed whole villages.

As the year 1347 went on, more and more stories began to circulate in England of terrible things happening abroad; merchants who traded with Bordeaux heard that France was now infected. The following summer, on June 23, 1348—St. John's Eve, a flirting and fertility festival, the only day of the year when unmarried women could act in a risqué manner by dancing with men—a ship carrying the disease turned up in Melcombe in Dorset. Within a decade, England had lost between a third and half of its population.

The Rootless Phantom

The first sign of the dreaded illness was bad breath, though at the time most oral hygiene probably wasn't at the highest standard to begin with. Then the afflicted suffered huge black growths on their armpits and groins before being struck down by a fever. Most victims would have four or five days of agonizing pain, after which between 60 and 90 percent would die.

To make matters more confusing to people with a limited knowledge of medical science, the disease came in three different forms, each of them ghastly although slightly different. The most common was bubonic plague, in which tumors the size of apples—inflamed lymphatic glands known as bubo—appeared on the neck, armpits, and groin, after which you were gone within a week.

Bubonic plague was transmitted by flea bites; the second type, pneumonic, spread through the air and contracted by breathing, was much more contagious and killed within forty-eight hours; in the Manchurian epidemic of 1921, life expectancy for people with pneumonic plague was 1.8 days. Then there was the septicaemic version, which took place when bubonic and pneumonic plague infected the blood and led to internal hemorrhaging. This caused dark blotches across the body known as 'God's tokens,' and killed even more quickly, often within hours, although it was much less common. The Florentine poet Boccaccio wrote: 'How many brave men, how many fair ladies, how many gallant youths, whom any physician, were he Galen, Hippocrates or Aesculapius himself, would have pronounced in the soundest of health, broke fast with their kinfolk, comrades and friends in the morning, and when evening came, supped with their forefathers in the other world!' Simon of Covino wrote of priests who 'were seized by the [P]lague whilst administering spiritual aid; and, often by a single touch, or a single breath of the Plague-stricken, perished even before the sick person they had come to assist.'

The disease also caused intoxication of the nervous system, which led to depression and a sort of madness, just to add to the general apocalyptic air. According to *The Black Death* author Philip Ziegler: 'In Provence a man climbed on to the roof of his house and threw down the tiles into the street. Another executed a mad, grotesque dance on the roof.'[3]

People who were infected developed blood that was black and thick, and sometimes 'thin green scum' rose to the surface, which usually suggested the end was near: 'Everything that issued from body, breath, sweat, blood from lungs and boils, bloody urine and bloody feces—smelled foul' and after a while 'death is seen seated on the face.'[4]

'Many died of boils and abscesses, and pustules on their legs and under their armpits; others frantic with pain in their head, and others spitting blood,' wrote an Irish friar unfortunate enough to live at the time.

Over the course of 1349, the Plague spread across England, averaging a mile a day, and the death rates were apocalyptic in parts. Jarrow in County Durham, for instance, lost 80 percent of its population, but this was not by any means the worst. In the manor of Wakefield, it was recorded that the village of Shelf 'is dead,' while at the abbot of Eynsham's manor of Tilgarsely in 1359, it was reported that they couldn't raise tax in the village because it had been empty since 1350, and this was not a small or poor settlement beforehand. In Cuxham in Oxfordshire, every one of twelve tenant farmers died in 1349, and four of eight cottagers. In Winchester, six parish churches were abandoned. The Plague led to ghost villages—some three thousand in England—although many were killed off not just by the actual disease but by peasants fleeing for better wages that followed, while in others there were clearances afterward as unprofitable humans were replaced by sheep.

With churchyards unable to cope, huge plague pits were built;[5] sometimes the living were thrown in with the dead, and the piles of corpses were seen to squirm from the movements of the dying. Mass burials had to be carried out with not enough living to bury the dead, while many also abandoned bodies, or dying family members, so terrified were they of the disease.

Over 1348–9, half of London's fifty thousand people died, while the death toll in Paris was up to eighty thousand out of a population of 150,000. When a village became infected, a black flag was flown over the parish church, and there were often so many corpses that church graveyards would stink from a great distance. The Plague was likened to 'black smoke' or a 'rootless phantom,'[6] and many quite reasonably thought it was the end of the world.

King Edward was asked to stay in the city of London to help with morale; his exact reply has never been recorded, but it was something to the effect of 'get stuffed.' However, even the royal family was affected by the disease: the king's daughter Joanne died of it on her way to Castile to marry Pedro the Cruel, although as he ended up later murdering his wife, perhaps she dodged a bullet.

Desperate for some divine help, the monarch wrote to Archbishop of Canterbury John Stratford in September 1348, asking him to put together some special national prayers. Unfortunately, as it turned out, the archbishop had died of the Plague over a week earlier. His successor, John de Ufford, lasted just six months before also succumbing to the pestilence; after him came Thomas Bradwardine, who perished from the disease within six weeks.

For a very few people, however, the Plague was a stroke of luck. At Eynsham Abbey in Oxfordshire, Abbot Nicholas was deprived of his office for some unrecorded wrongdoing. Bishop Gynewell nominated two administrators to run the abbey before a new man could be found, but they soon both died, and so the two monks who brought the news were given their jobs instead. However, both men were dead before they even reached the Abbey, and so Abbot Nicholas got the job back.

The Scots mockingly called the disease 'the foul death of England . . . God's judgment on the English' and seeing that their neighbor was weakened, they decided to invade in 1349, with predictable results. Their forces amassed in Selkirk, 'laughing at their enemies,' and were about to swarm across the border when 'the fearful mortality fell upon them and the Scots were scattered by sudden and savage death so that, within a short period, some five thousand died.'[7] The soldiers went home, dying on the road and spreading the disease to their homes, as they lamented from the 'foule deth that Ynglessh men dyene upon.'

In Ireland, Friar John Clyn of Kilkenny described rather gloomily, 'waiting among the dead for the coming of death. I have committed to writing those things that I have truly heard and seen, and lest the work of recording perish together with the writer, I leave parchment just in case any human survivor should remain who might wish to continue the work that I have begun.' He died soon after, rather justified in his pessimism.

Almost everywhere in Europe the same story was repeated, although Italy was the worst affected with maybe two-thirds of the population wiped out. Gherado, brother of the famous poet Petrarch, was one of thirty-six members of a Carthusian monastery at the onset of the Plague—and the only one left afterwards.

Every day he buried as many as three of his fellow monks 'until he was left alone with his dog and fled to look for a place that would take him in.'

Because of the Plague, Siena Cathedral, which would have been the most enormous in the world, was never finished, although it looks fairly spectacular as it is. Florence was the worst affected with well over half of its population killed; its great historian Giovannni Villani died in mid-sentence, writing 'in the midst of this pestilence there came to an end . . . ' before succumbing.

The period was also marked by a number of other freakish disasters, which reinforced the idea that someone up there didn't like them. A tidal wave destroyed much of Cyprus and despite the people trying to flee to the hills, 'a pestiferous wind spread so poisonous an odour that many, being overpowered by it, fell down suddenly and expired in dreadful agonies.'[8]

In some parts of Europe, such as Dubrovnik, wolves walked into towns and ate corpses openly; in others, the animals shied away from humans, fearful of their disease.

Scandinavia was infected via England; it was brought to Norway by a ship in May 1349, in which someone had come aboard already ill and while at sea the whole crew died. The empty boat drifted toward Bergen like a scene straight from a Werner Herzog film, the unsuspecting locals going aboard before they realized what had killed the passengers.[9] Some Swedes fled from civilization in order to build a mountain hideaway in a new town called Tusededal, but the Plague followed, and from their sanctuary just one girl survived, discovered years later and shunning human company. She was christened Rype, or 'wild bird,' but eventually returned to normal and married; in fact her family, the Rypes, were still big land owners in the area centuries later.

In Avignon, where the papacy had been situated since 1309, one graveyard received eleven thousand corpses in six weeks, and so many people died that the pope had the Rhone River consecrated so people could just chuck the bodies in without worrying about their souls.

Not every region suffered equally; Bohemia and Poland were almost entirely unaffected, partly because the king of Poland had closed the border but also because that part of Europe was off the beaten track. Milan had a far lower death rate than most cities because its exceptionally cruel ruler Luchino Visconti (later poisoned by his wife) acted with ruthless efficiency: when the disease was first discovered, all the occupants of the three houses affected were walled up and left to die. The Duke of Milan also decreed anyone who brought the Plague into the city was subject to the death penalty, which seems a bit unnecessary; Plague victims were otherwise taken out of the city to die or recover in the fields. Meanwhile, in Venice, beggars were banned from displaying corpses in the streets, 'as was their macabre custom.'

Generally, people in the cities had a far higher death rate due to greater human contact but also because of the squalor. The population of England had tripled since the Norman Conquest, and this led to filthy, overcrowded towns filled with rat-friendly wood and straw buildings. As one author put it: 'The medieval house might have been built to specifications approved by a rodent council as eminently suitable for the rat's enjoyment of a healthy and carefree life.'[10]

Cities really were disgusting most of the time; in 1307, the Palace of Westminster had a pipe that carried waste out through a sewer but this was probably unique, and most excrement was just thrown into a ditch or the street. The River Fleet, a tributary of the Thames to the west of London, was so choked by the filth from eleven latrines and three sewers that parts of it did not flow due to the buildup. In London, rakers occasionally threw the city's filth into great pits outside the city or in the river, but that was about the extent of sanitary policy, while the streets were filled with rotting animal heads, offal, and fish.

London was so disgusting people would pipe their waste into the unused cellars of unsuspecting neighbors, as the Assize of Nuisances discovered in 1347 when one such basement overflowed; or they dug cesspools in their yards and constructed DIY latrines. One fourteenth-century Londoner, Roger the Raker, did this so often that the pit filled to capacity and began to rot the floorboards, and on one visit he unfortunately plunged through the floorboards and drowned in his own excrement. Probably not how he envisioned his life turning out. Sewage and drinking water were often in close proximity with obviously negative results, and tanners' and dyers' waste also went into the water supply. It was little wonder that people chose to drink alcohol instead.

In 1300, Edward I had ordered the people of Oxford to clean up their town because, he complained, 'the air is so corrupted and infected that an abominable loathing [is] diffused among the foresaid masters and scholars.' His grandson would introduce rules about hygiene in London, restricting certain activities in the city, and banishing trades to outposts such as Knightsbridge. And progress was being made: public latrines were in London and in a handful of other cities, and fresh water pipes were also in London, Exeter, Southampton, and Bristol.

Health at the time was not great anyway. Lots of people had skin diseases, for example, and eye infections were also common; animals lived with people, and clothes were rarely washed. Remains of Plague victims in London showed that many had suffered from malnutrition and around one in six had rickets—the bone disease caused by lack of vitamins—a problem that had increased in previous centuries due to population pressure.

Across Western Europe, the previous population boom was now reversed, and many areas would not recover their pre-Plague levels until centuries later.[11] When Kenneth Clark went to film the BBC2 television series *Civilisation* in Sienna, he was told the population was less than its pre-Plague levels by two people.

Theories

In October 1348, the king of France asked the leading thinkers at the University of Paris for their theories about what was causing the disease. Putting together all their knowledge, wisdom, and studies, the doctors concluded that it was all down to 'a triple conjunction of Saturn, Jupiter, and Mars in the 40th degree of Aquarius' that took place on March 20, 1345, because a conjunction of Saturn and Jupiter always brought disaster and Mars and Jupiter together meant plague. Well it's a theory, and it became the official explanation accepted across the continent, even in Muslim Spain.[12]

Medical science had hardly improved since classical Greece; surgery was also seen as low-grade manual labor, and touching naked bodies was viewed as beneath the dignity of a cleric; this is why surgeons in Britain are today not doctors but mere misters. The most important anatomist of the age, John of Ardene, who 'made important contributions to the treatment of gout, clysters, and fistula,' learned everything from being an army surgeon in the Hundred Years' War, where the one thing they weren't short of was dead bodies.[13]

Across Europe it was believed that 'bad drove out bad' so people took to inhaling unpleasant odors to rid themselves of the horrible-smelling plague. Contemporary doctor John Colle believed that '[a]ttendants who take care of latrines and those who serve in hospitals and other malodorous places are nearly all to be considered immune.' As a result, 'it was not unknown for apprehensive citizens of a plague-struck city to spend hours each day crouched over a latrine absorbing with relish the foetid smells.'[14]

Other remedies, in the words of one historian, 'have a certain antiquarian charm but you would not want to undergo them.'[15] A handbook for doctors at St. Bart's in London recommended women's milk sucked directly from the breast, and if no lactating women were available then asses' or goats' milk should work. How the women felt about having Plague victims fondling their breasts is never explained; the donkeys probably weren't that ecstatic either, for that matter. Also advised was having a bath with the head entirely covered and chest wrapped in the skin of a small goat, which probably couldn't do much harm.

It wasn't until the nineteenth century that humans learned the cause of bubonic plague—rats and their plague-carrying fleas—and it's quite reasonable to be confused, as the disease-carrying fleas could survive forty days without a rat.

Whatever the fancy theories of the eggheads at Paris University, most people thought the obvious answer was that the 'Great Mortality,' as they called it, was caused by God's anger. Contemporaries saw all sorts of omens to confirm this: a column of fire was spotted above the papal palace at Avignon, a ball of flames above Paris, a stranded whale, mysterious bloodstains on men's clothes that turned out to be butterfly excrement. There was a small earthquake in Hull in December 1348, followed by the birth of conjoined twins nearby.

The pope decreed that a penitent procession be held in which many people would meet to atone for their sins, with groups of up to two thousand getting together, the unfortunate but predictable result being that a lot of them got the Plague.

Inevitably, many blamed the disaster on loose morals, and such abominations as men dressing in sexually provocative clothes, so that 'from the back the wearers look more like women than men.' Others attacked bodily adornments, such as full doublets 'cutted on the buttok,' which 'inflame women with lecherous desires.' They also looked at such manifestations of decadence as tournaments, where women were dressed in 'the most sumptuous male costumes,' tight trouser-wearing female cheerleaders at jousts seen as indicative of Edward III's dubious morals.

The misanthropic chronicler Henry Knighton wrote that they 'wearied their bodies with fooleries and wanton buffoonery . . . But God, in this matter, as in all others, brought marvellous remedy.'

Knighton, it's fair to say, was pretty reactionary even by the standards of the day, and most people thought God had gone too far this time.

Much of the new fashion for racier, more sexualized clothing came down to a simple thirteenth-century invention, the button, which allowed clothes to be more figure-hugging and therefore emphasize masculine or feminine body parts.

Across the water, John of Bridlington blamed the Plague on the king of France and his 'avarice, luxury, envy, gluttony, and anger,' which in fairness was an accurate description of his personality. King Philippe responded to the disease with laws against blasphemy; for the first offense a man would lose a lip, for the second the other lip, and for the third the tongue. London guilds also banned apprentices from cutting their hair 'like a gallant or a man of court,' while the Siena city council banned gambling 'forever' in June 1348, although this led to such a loss of revenue that 'forever' turned out to be 'until the end of the year.' Dice across Italy were banned and so dice makers instead moved to selling religious knickknacks.

Morality laws were also introduced in the city of Tournai in Flanders, so men and women living together were ordered to marry at once. Swearing, playing dice, and working on Sundays were all banned; no bells were to be rung at funerals, no mourning clothes worn, and no wakes held.

The strangest consequence of the Black Death was the rise of the Flagellant movement, in which groups of hundreds of people moved from town to town dressed in sackcloth and whipped themselves. The Brotherhood of the Cross, as the movement was called, seemed to emerge spontaneously and involved large groups of men stripped to the waist, 'scourging themselves with leather whips tipped with iron spikes until they bled.'[16] They cried out 'Spare us!' to God and Christ and the people cried in sympathy; they'd do three times a day, and it would go on for thirty-three and a half days to symbolize Christ's time on earth. Members weren't allowed to wash, shave, talk, change their clothes, or sleep in bed without their master's permission, and they were also supposed to adopt celibacy, although they were also accused of having orgies.

Collective self-harming sessions would start with each member rhythmically beating their chests and backs with a scourge, an instrument that had three or four metal-studded leather thongs attached, all the while being cheered on by a crowd and their master. The onlookers would encourage them by singing the Hymn of the Flagellants, until eventually the fanatical self-harmers would throw themselves to the ground before reaching a crescendo of mortification.

This insanity swept through Germany, the Low Countries, and Northern France, becoming larger and increasingly hysterical until, inevitably, they became violent, in particular against the Catholic hierarchy. Church leaders tried to stop the group but whenever priests got in their way they were assaulted or killed. Some Flagellants came to London in 1349, whipping themselves outside St. Paul's—where they were received with stony silence by the mystified English who presumably just found the whole thing so embarrassing.

It came amid an atmosphere of increased hostility toward authority generally, but the mob soon moved on to a more obvious target, and soon an epidemic of anti-Semitic pogroms swept across Europe. At first, people blamed lepers for the Plague, and victims of the disease were banned from entering the city of London because they were accused of trying to 'contaminate others with that abominable blemish' through 'their polluted breath, as by carnal intercourse with women in stews and other secret places.' Lepers had always been the object of suspicion, and, in 1321 in Languedoc, all the lepers were accused of poisoning wells, bribed to do so by the Jews on behalf of the Muslim king of Granada. Why or how these three totally disparate, random groups could have gotten together to hatch this scheme no one thought to properly explain.

But people believed some quite outlandish theories. One Polish historian, Dlugoss, thought the Jews had managed to poison the air with Plague, while many thought Jews were working for the leader of Muslim Spain, and that powdered poison was imported in large quantities from the East. However, the main conspiracy theory involved Jews poisoning the water supply.

Suspicion was partly aroused because Jews often did drink from open streams rather than from dirty wells, as Jewish ideas about hygiene were a bit further advanced due to their religious rules. A Swiss chronicler noted that Jews knew wells to be full of 'bad, noxious moistures and vapours' and there were even recorded incidences of them warning gentile neighbors to avoid the wells because they were so filthy, for all the thanks they got.

The first big massacres took place in Languedoc in the south of France, followed by Strasbourg where two thousand people were killed in a riot, with pogroms on a scale that would not be seen again until the twentieth century. The pope denounced the persecution and repeatedly attacked the rumors, pointing out that Jews were dying in large numbers from the disease, too, but the mob could not be controlled.

Only in England was there no massacre of the Jews, mainly because there were none left after Edward I had persecuted them.[17]

Social Impact

Whether or not loose morals had caused the Plague, they were certainly a result of it, as people reasoned that if they were going to die soon of a horrific disease they may as well have fun now. Churchman William Dene of Rochester complained that 'the entire population, or the greater part of it, has become even more depraved, even more prone to every kind of vice, more readily to indulge in evil and sinfulness, without a thought of death.' Another contemporary, John Gower, wrote a miserable book called *Vox Clamantis*, 'The Voice of One Crying Out,' in which 'he described how man grew increasingly feckless, corrupt and base, turning from God, obsessed by material gain, and ripe for divine punishment.'[18]

There was an increase in violence afterward and more maltreatment of orphans, while a greater number of people carried arms. People lived for the moment and acted impulsively. Crime also went up because there was little in the way of authority, especially since aristocrats had often fled from cities (which, in the case of Barcelona, emboldened mobs to attack Jews). In Italy, the Plague also unleashed the horrors of the *becchini*, Plague victims who conducted home invasions in which men were forced to hand over their possessions or be infected, and women were often assaulted.

Art and literature became much more morbid. Tombs, which used to show the dearly departed in their youth, now represented them as rotting skeletons, sometimes with worms popping out of their eyeholes. Archbishop of Canterbury Henry Chichele had his tomb finished twenty years before he died, using it as an interesting talking point with visitors when they came around. Even epitaphs were grimmer; Cardinal Jean de La Grange, who died in Avignon in 1402, had as his inscription: 'So, miserable one, what cause for pride?'

After the Plague, Church walls were painted with depictions of terrifying skeleton figures warning us of our eventual demise, most prominently Triani's fresco of 'The Three Living and Three Dead,' which shows a thirteenth-century legend about three young nobles who meet three decomposing corpses who tell them: 'What you are, we were. What we are, you will be.' A popular poem from 1376, the 'Dance Macabre,' featured the cheerful verses 'dead, naked, rotten and stinking. So will you be . . . everyone should think at least once a day of his loathsome end.'

Religious art became more focused on the more horrific stories of the Bible. The cult of St. Sebastian, for instance, which emphasized suffering and misery, became more popular, as did the story of Job, the character from the Old Testament for whom everything goes wrong in life because God feels like it. Among the most popular books of the later fourteenth century was Pope Innocent III's treatise, *On the Misery of the Human Condition*, written in 1195.

The general cultural atmosphere was one of despair. In the words of scholar-soldier Philippe de Mézières: 'The things of this fleeting world go for ever from bad to worse.' A monk at Cluny wrote: 'What can we think but that the whole human race, root and branch, is sliding willingly down again into the gulf of primeval chaos.'

The Plague returned in 1361, an outbreak known as the Mortality of the Children as it killed so many people born after 1348, who had no immunity. Records show that one in four heirs of estates died in that outbreak, compared to an overall death rate of 15 percent; a further plague year in 1369 killed another one in ten.

The Black Death would trouble Europe until the seventeenth century, when it died out because the black rat was driven out by its relative, the brown rat, which was stronger and less dependent on the wooden houses its cousin loved. Now all people had to worry about was smallpox.

CHAPTER EIGHT

The Black Prince

Meanwhile, the conflict between the English and French dragged on, the Plague hardly stopping the enthusiasm for war, even though the country was so broke that King Edward had resorted to alchemy, the optimistic medieval science of turning base metals into gold. He paid alchemist John de Walden five thousand crowns of king's gold and twenty pounds of silver 'to work thereon by the art of alchemy for the benefit of the king.' It didn't work, unfortunately, and de Walden was put in the Tower in 1350.

This failure did not put off the king of France trying the exact same thing in 1365, when he summoned to his court Thomas of Pisano, a doctor of astrology from the University of Bologna. Thomas was already controversial because the medicine he gave the monarch was full of mercury, which is poisonous, but his plan was ingenious: 'Out of lead and tin, he fashioned hollow images of nude men, filled them with earth collected from the center and four corners of France, inscribed the foreheads with the names of King Edward or one of his captains, and, when the constellations were right, buried them facedown while he recited spells to the effect that this was perpetual expulsion, annihilation, and burial of the said King, captains, and all adherents.'[1] Remarkably, this didn't work.

The English king was forced to raise taxes to support the war, and, in 1346, he tried to float a new international currency, a sterling bloc valid both in England and Flanders, but it failed, as these sort of pan-national European currencies tend to. Edward also helped the continent to have a huge banking crisis, as if it didn't have enough troubles. Edward borrowed 1.5 million gold florins from the Bardi and Peruzzi family, the great Italian bankers, and his inability to pay them back led to the first great European banking crash in the 1340s. Almost all the bankers, Italian and Dutch, who lent Edward money for the war, went bankrupt at some point.

England's economy was dependent on wool, and it was so prized that the Italians had words for places such as Sirisestri, Guincestri, and Ghondisqualdo—Cirencester, Winchester, and the Cotswolds. By 1300, England was exporting twelve million woolen fleeces annually,[2] and the country's eighteen million sheep accounted for two-thirds of crown income via a tax on wool; this was collected by just one hundred agents (three-quarters of them unpaid). Defending the wool industry was an added motivation for the war and it was so important that Edward ordered that the lord chancellor in Parliament sit on a bale of wool to symbolize why Crecy was fought; the seat of the lord speaker in the House of Lords is still called the woolsack. In order to fund the war, Edward had borrowed thirteen thousand pounds from a Hull wool merchant called William de la Pole, whose children and grandchildren would rise to become a powerful aristocratic family in the following century and almost took the throne, although William never got a penny of his money back.

In 1350, the Castilians, allies of the French, assembled at Sluys to attack England. Edward gathered his ships at Sandwich and, accompanied by his ten-year-old son John, went to meet the enemy on board the *Thomas*, the same ship he had been on at Sluys ten years earlier. According to Froissart, 'the king stood at his ship's prow, clad in a jacket of black velvet, and on his head a hat of black beaver that became him right well; and he was then (as I was told by such as were with him that day) as merry as ever he was seen.' Whatever the rights and wrongs of the war, he pulled off the look; on board Edward made the minstrels play a German dance and forced his commander John Chandos to sing with them.

Philippe VI had died in 1350 to be replaced by his nice but ineffectual son Jean II, regarded as one of the dimmest men to ever rule France. The war was prolonged by the intrigue and violence at the French court, which was now entering its Renaissance era of sexual depravity, poisoning, and hereditary insanity. The most notorious aristocrat was the king's cousin Charles of Navarre, known as Charles the Bad, and with good reason, having murdered one of King Jean's favorites, Charles of Spain, in 1354. Navarre then entered an alliance with the English in Gascony before inevitably double-crossing them.

Navarre was suspected of plotting to seize power, a conspiracy that was rumored to include the Dauphin, also confusingly called Charles.[3] So on April 5, 1356, while the two Charleses and some Norman allies were having a banquet, the king turned up in full armor with soldiers and had them all arrested. Four Norman lords were immediately executed, and the king besieged rebel strongholds in Normandy. While this was all going on the English were preparing to invade.

Free Companies

Warfare was increasingly becoming a business done by professionals, and much of the fighting was carried out not by the king's soldiers, but terrifying mercenary groups called the Free Companies. Such armies had existed since the twelfth century and were notorious for living on plunder, murder, and rape, but they were more effective and professional than most conventional forces, which were led by aristocrats who were often more interested in showing off than in achieving any actual military objective.

In France these Free Companies were called *ecorcheurs* (skinners) and *routiers*—highwaymen—while in Italy they were known as *condottieri* or 'contract men.' There were different types of Free Companies, and some were highly organized with their own uniform, like the *bandes blanches* worn by followers of the notorious 'Archpriest' Arnaud de Cervole, a dreadful former clergyman who ended up being lynched by his own troops. Many mercenary leaders came to terrible ends: Seguin de Badefol was poisoned by Charles the Bad for asking for money he was owed, while another former cleric, Friar Jean Monreale, who at his peak could command 150,000 gold florins to fight for Venice against Milan, was executed in Rome, where he went to his death magnificently dressed and totally unrepentant declaring he had carved 'his way with a sword through a false and miserable world.'

There were 106 free companies in total, mostly led by roguish aristocrats with the ranks filled with medieval England's dregs, outlaws, and general losers. Sir Robert Knollys, one of the first *routiers*, or rutters as they were called in England, was principal captain of the Grand Company in 1358 and made seventeen thousand pounds or so in one year, making him equivalent to a multi-multi-millionaire.[4] At one point, he controlled forty castles in the Loire Valley, and was so feared it was said peasants threw themselves in rivers whenever his name was mentioned; eventually, he even threatened the pope himself at Avignon. Edward III gave Knollys an official pardon for beating the French despite all the numerous horrific crimes he'd committed, and he ended up as his chief of staff, dying a rich and happy man in 1407.

Another mercenary leader was Knollys's half brother Sir Hugh Calveley, who led two thousand routiers on a rampage through Armagnac in southwest France in the 1360s. He also had to be pardoned for a felony, but ended up deputy lieutenant of Calais and then governor of Brest in Brittany. Another, Sir Robert Salle, was a Norfolk serf who went on to be knighted for his courage; however, in 1381, after returning home he was murdered in Essex by envious peasants—a surprisingly common problem for people who rose up. These companies collected vast amounts of plunder; one led by Sir John Harleston drank out of one hundred chalices they had looted from the churches of Champagne. As the pope said in his 1364 excommunication against the mercenaries, these companies were 'Unbridled in every kind of cruelty; they were another plague.'

To make matters worse, the professional soldiers grouped themselves into an even bigger and more dangerous unit, the so-called Grand Company, which, in 1361, got to Avignon and held the pope at ransom. They were so out of control that the Holy Father organized a Crusade to fight the mercenaries, but he would not pay the Crusaders who arrived in Provence, offering only indulgences—that is 'spiritual' payment—so they left as soon as they arrived. In fact, some went to join the mercenaries they were supposed to be fighting. The pope ended up paying the brigands one hundred thousand florins along with a general pardon if they left, encouraging them to move onto Italy, to cap off a fantastic century for the Italians.

At the time, Italy was divided between various squabbling city-states, among them Milan, Genoa, Florence, and Pisa. Because they were wealthy, the Italian aristocracy had long since hired mercenaries to do their work and had no experience of soldiering, preferring other people to do it. In Lombardy 'nothing was more terrible to hear than the name of the English,' who were *perfidi e scelleratissimi* (perfidious and most wicked), although it was conceded that 'they did not roast and mutilate their victims like the Hungarians.'[5] Piedmont chronicler Pietro Azario wrote that 'some men imprisoned themselves in their own dungeons and locked themselves up at night' when the English turned up.

The most notorious mercenary was Sir John Hawkwood, or as they called him in Italy, Giovanni Acuto, 'Sharp John.' He had entered Edward's army as a lowly soldier, but by 1360 he was in charge of his own free company, the Tard-Venus; two years later he took a new mercenary super group, the White Company, into Italy and ended up being paid a fortune by Florence in what was effectively a protection racket. He eventually married an illegitimate daughter of the Duke of Milan. Once asked why he didn't try encouraging peace, he replied: 'Do you not know that I live by war and that peace would be my undoing?'

The mercenary groups were officially disowned by the English crown, but secretly encouraged, although some aristocrats hated the way that the Free Companies represented the commercialization of warfare when for them it was all about fighting for its own sake. And the next great battle in particular would signal the beginning of the end for the aristocratic order, with a second, even greater Plantagenet victory at Poitiers in 1356 where seven thousand Englishmen led by the king's son defeated up to thirty-five thousand French.

That year, the Black Prince had gone on a rampage through the southwest of France, with twenty-six hundred men-at-arms, spending two months destroying the region of Languedoc and burning down the cities of Carcassonne and Narbonne in a six-hundred-mile trail of carnage. So terrifying were the English that many took to hiding in caves and forests, and the prince wrote back to his father, satisfied of the 'many goodly towns and strongholds burnt and destroyed.'

Eventually, Edward was caught by a much larger French force and found himself too far away from Gascony to escape; he tried to negotiate his way out of it, and to make things worse the English had run out of provisions three days earlier. Yet, against incredible odds they won, as the French cavalry was once again outdone by archers, who were lethally effective while the noblemen were too busy competing to see who could get the most glory in battle by being in the middle; Poitiers more than any other battle represented the end of the supremacy of cavalry.

For the winners it was a bonanza in human prizes, and many English soldiers had four, five, or even six prisoners, so many captured they could not drag them all back and had to release some on the condition that they promised to come to Bordeaux with their ransoms before Christmas. Once they had looted everything, the English rabble took their winnings back to Gascony where 'they spent foolishly all the gold and silver they had won' on booze and women. Among the winners, the Earl of Warwick got eight thousand pounds for taking the Archbishop of Sens, while a squire who captured the bishop of Le Mans got one thousand pounds by selling him to Edward.

Most humiliating of all, King Jean himself was captured and the hapless monarch was transported back first to Gascony, where he was complimented on his fighting by his hosts/jailors who were 'laden with gold, silver, and prisoners.' Edward now had two kings as his personal prisoners, as the Scots were too poor to pay the ransom for King David. Afterwards, Jean was taken to London where, during a procession that lasted hours, he rode through the city on a white horse showered with golden leaves by beautiful maidens hired by the city guilds. At a feast, the English toasted and honored him as a great and brave king, with the Black Prince waiting on him at the table, an example of the sometimes elaborate nature of chivalry.

The laws of chivalry meant that aristocrats had a far better chance of surviving a battle because they were worth a lot of money as prisoners; not so much if you were common soldiers. Sir Robert Knolles went into battle with an inscription attached that read 'Whoever captures Sir Robert Knolles will gain 100,000 moutons,' a *mouton d'or* being worth one-third of a pound of silver, a fair amount of money.

The code also did occasionally reduce the amount of killing. In 1351, an English garrison at Ploermel was attacked by a French force, so in order to avoid a slaughter they agreed to have a fight between thirty of each of their best men. This Combat of the Thirty, in which the French won, became the stuff of legend, with poems being written about it, and anyone who fought that day was feted;

no doubt the number of people who took part in the Combat of the Thirty magically ballooned into the thousands.

Things continued to go disastrously for France and it was ridden with the usual infighting and, worse still, began to see rural violence. Charles the Bad, who had been put in a dungeon in the Louvre, escaped in 1357 and, along with a Parisian demagogue called Etienne Marcel, set up a revolutionary government in charge of the capital. As with that much later French exercise in people power, it was always going to end badly.

The French and English, meanwhile, had countless peace negotiations, which almost stopped the war dragging on. In 1358, a deal was rejected by the Paris Estates-General, and just to emphasize the point the 'Paris mob invaded the royal palace, battered his ministers to death before his [the dauphin's] eyes, and flung their corpses from an upper window.'[6] Which was a no.

That year there erupted the *Jacquerie*, a huge rural uprising across France, so called because of the *jacques*, clothing worn by peasants (from which we get jacket). There were stories of women being forced to eat their roasted husband's flesh before being tortured to death along with their children, and it was only put down with fierce brutality, leaving tens of thousands dead. New peace talks in 1359 failed, and so Edward III landed at Calais in October with ten thousand men, the monarch now pushing fifty. It turned out to be a grim adventure for the English, followed by French cavalry who would pick off stragglers. That year happened to have an extremely harsh winter with torrential rain turning the roads into swamps, mud-filled overflowing rivers, and undrinkable water, and the English also ran out of food but dared not go foraging. Among those on the tour of 1359–1360 was a young Geoffrey Chaucer, who was taken prisoner in Brittany and ransomed for sixteen pounds. He later wrote: 'There is ful many a man that crieth "Werre! Werrre!" that wote ful litel what werre amounteth.' He obviously did not have a good time.

In January 1360, the English, now rather aimless, arrived in upper Burgundy and drank three thousand butts (four thousand liters) of wine, and the local duke paid them thirty-three thousand pounds to leave. However, after Winchester was raided in March widespread panic was in England, even though this tiny attack was nothing compared to what the English had inflicted on France. In October 1360, with two-thirds of the first installment of ransom paid, the English allowed King Jean to return home, but he had to leave three sons as hostages. The French raised some of the money by selling the king's eleven-year-old daughter to the son of the notorious Duke of Milan, Gian Galeazzo Visconti, one of the richest and most immoral men in the world.

A peace treaty was finally agreed to in 1361, known as the *clause c'estassavoir*—'that is to say'—because in it Edward was to renounce his claim to France while simultaneously Jean would renounce Gascony, but for complicated reasons these two sub-clauses were set aside with the understanding that it would all be formalized later. However later it would all unravel. The English couldn't even enforce much of the treaty anyway because they had lost control of the thousands of hooligans running around France, who refused to hand over as many as 150 castles to the French.

In 1364, while more negotiations were going on, one of Jean's sons left England to rejoin his wife, and so the king felt obliged to go back to London to take his place, where he received a great reception, the English admiring his honesty. In fact, his reception was so good that all the parties and banquettes they held in his honor soon finished him off, Jean dying of overindulgence aged just forty-four. The English held a grand requiem at St. Paul's for the king they'd accidently killed before the body was returned to Paris.

The Last Days of Edward III

The war ground to a halt and the last days of Edward III were very depressing for everyone. The economy declined, and it was during this period that Robin Hood first appeared in written form, although it originally dated to some point in the thirteenth century (the connection with the reign of Richard the Lionheart, in the 1190s, was not made until far later). The great story of the time, Piers Plowman, told the adventures of a lowly peasant who liked to grumble about the powers that be; its author William Langland had once been employed to sing songs for rich men's souls. Plowman has an explicitly political message at a time when the poor were growing agitated at the rich, the senile old king, the selfish barons, and the local gentry who were trying to enforce pre-Plague wages. Other popular songs and poems paint a similar scene; the 'Song of the Husbandman' from around 1340 tells the story of a poor farm-worker being taken by officials: 'I sold my seed to seek silver for the king, wherefore my land lies fallow and learns to sleep.'

English fortunes in war went badly from 1364. After Jean II died, the new king Charles V was a far more effective enemy, even though he was afflicted by numerous ailments including ulcers and an 'undiagnosed disease which frequently sent him exhausted to bed.' He was a true intellectual with an interest in history and theology, and had twelve hundred chained books kept in a tower at the Louvre.

The English continued to pursue ever more pointless military adventures. The Black Prince became involved in a civil war in Castile, but while he initially won in 1369, his ally Pedro the Cruel was thrown out and his 'sole tangible gain was a great "ruby"—actually a garnet—once the property of the Sultan of Granada,' which is still part of the English crown jewels.[7]

The Black Prince had been put in charge of Gascony, whose people quickly became resentful of his interference, and, in 1369, the peace fell apart when Edward was summoned to do homage by the king of France. He refused and Aquitaine was formally confiscated; Edward III resumed the title King of France again and they were back to square one. The Black Prince said he'd answer the summons to Paris with a helmet on his head and an army behind it. Unfortunately, he was now bedridden after contracting dropsy (today called edema, a buildup of fluids beneath the skin) while on campaign in Castile, which meant he basically spent ten years dying in agony.

In 1370, English military leader John Chandos was killed when he marched toward a French force with three hundred men, slipped on dewy ground, and was struck by an enemy sword on the side of his head, going into his brain. That same year, Sir Robert Knollys was put in charge of an army, but many English lords refused to serve 'the old bandit' and so they went off. He led yet another pointless rampage that reached the outskirts of Paris, and ended with the French king wisely refusing to fight them.

In August that year, the Black Prince was carried by bearers in a litter on campaign during his last great trip through France. He was overseeing the siege of Limoges, and after it fell he ordered the execution of three thousand men, women, and children, which Froissart called 'a most melancholy business.' The three leaders of the garrison survived because they had fought against John of Gaunt and two other English leaders, and so under the rules of chivalry they could not be executed. Limoges was nearly Edward's last act 'for always his sickness increased,' and, further depressed by the death of his eldest son in 1372, he resigned the principality of Aquitaine and retired to Berkhamsted, near London, where he lived out the last few miserable years of his life.

In 1373, Gaunt led a new *chevauchée* that took in Picardy, Champagne, Burgundy, the Bourbonnais, the Auvergne, and Limousin, filled with the usual criminals. Of the eleven thousand men who started out, only six thousand reached Bordeaux, and pretty much all the horses died on the way. It was quite an achievement from a technical point of view, but in another sense utterly pointless, and they didn't capture a single town.

By now, some Englishmen had openly condemned the war on moral grounds. In *De Officio Regis*, Oxford cleric John Wycliffe said warfare was contrary to the Ten Commandments, while Dominican John Bromyard wrote in *Summa Praedicantium* that the conflict had led to contempt for life and greed.

Edward's last few years were personally sad. The king, suffering from dysentery, paid 134 pounds for a quack treatment of 'ambergris, musk, pears, gold, and silver,' which cost the equivalent of three knights' yearly income. Unsurprisingly, it did not work. Later, he had a series of strokes that weakened his mind as well as his body, and became a 'foolish, infatuated old man . . . not stronger in mind than a boy of eight,' and was also drunk most of the time. The queen died in 1369, ending her many years as a positive influence on her husband (she is also the first queen of whom we have a good likeness, reflecting the increasing extent that we are entering the Renaissance). As well as her famous clemency at Calais, Philippa saved the lives of carpenters who were blamed for the Cheapside tournament disaster in 1331 when a stadium stand had collapsed and killed several people 'to the . . . embarrassment of knights and ladies of the Court'; the natural response of the king was to execute everyone involved.

Edward now came under the sway of his mistress, Alice Perrers, giving her his wife's robes and jewels with which she paraded through London while on a triumphal chariot under the title of 'Lady of the Sun.' It was even alleged she had given him gonorrhea, although considering his sexual history it could have been anyone. Perrers was widely hated and, in 1376, the 'Good Parliament,' as it was called—different parliamentary sessions went by nicknames at the time—decided enough was enough, and elected their first speaker to limit the abuses of courtiers, a role that still exists in the Commons and the US House of Representatives. One knight, Peter De La Mare, gave an interesting speech, and so he was chosen.

De La Mare declared that the king 'has with him certain councilors and servants who are not loyal or profitable to him or the kingdom' and so the process of impeachment was invented, whereby public officials were now answerable not just to the king but to public representatives; impeachment was abolished in Britain in the nineteenth century, but is still in existence in the United States.

The Good Parliament demanded redress of 146 grievances before they would give any more money, including dismissing corrupt ministers and Perrers, who was widely believed to be a witch. It was the first time the House of Commons attacked the crown, for Edward had always managed to keep Parliament and lords on his side, although there were disagreements. He disliked lawyers in particular and, on seven occasions from 1330 to 1372, lawyers and 'maintainers of quarrels' were excluded from sitting as county representatives in Parliament. His grandson Henry IV took it further by banning all lawyers from Parliament in 1404.

In June that year, Edward the Black Prince passed away and the following summer the ailing king joined him. As he lay dying, his mistress—'that unspeakable whore' as the somewhat unsympathetic chronicler Thomas Walsingham called her—supposedly pulled the ring from his finger to sell it.

The obituary of Edward III at Westminster Abbey read: 'Here lies the glory of England, the paragon of past kings, the model of future ones . . . the unconquered leopard.' That was how he was seen, and it is only because William Shakespeare wrote a play about Henry V that Edward was edged out as the country's number one military hero; for a long while, people harked after the glory days of his reign, rather overlooking the endless bloodshed and plague, because the nation was united, feared, and famous even 'in heathennesse and Barbary.'[8]

Edward was regarded as the pinnacle of military virtue, but he also left his country in a perilous state. The elderly, drunk king may not have noticed, but it was bubbling with tension.

In 1377, poet John Gower had said:

> he who observes the present time
> is likely to fear that soon . . .

this impatient nettle [the people]
will very suddenly sting us.[9]

England was about to erupt.

CHAPTER NINE

The Peasants' Revolt

On June 21, 1377, the guild masters of London rode into the Black Prince's former palace at Kennington just across the Thames from London, and swore their loyalty to the new king, his ten-year-old son Richard of Bordeaux.

A boy on the throne was a problem, and within weeks the French threatened to invade. Richard II's reign began with a series of military failures, and from the start it was ridden with division and the crown was bankrupt. Richard would become famous as a Shakespearean lunatic, but he had inherited a terrible mess and his enemies were mostly a dreadful bunch.

The most powerful was his uncle John of Gaunt, who had in the last years of his father's reign inherited the title of Duke of Lancaster from his father-in-law Henry (Lancaster was a county palatinate and therefore virtually self-governing). Gaunt was universally hated, and, in 1376, a London mob had almost killed him, while the common people believed all sorts of rumors circulating around, such as he poisoned his first wife, which is unlikely (divorce wasn't a big issue at the time because the chances were one spouse would die of some ghastly disease before too long).

To pay for the war, a new levy was imposed called a 'poll tax.' There had never been a universal tax before, and they soon learned why, for, in 1381, rural anger erupted into the biggest popular uprising in English history. The peasants were revolting.

Although the word was only coined in 1776 by Adam Smith, the social system at the time is generally known as feudalism, from *feodum*, old French for land. The term denotes a precapitalist society in which goods, services, and labor were not freely exchanged, but instead people were bound to one another by social obligations such as labor, with the king at the top and the serfs at the bottom.

Just below the monarch, the aristocracy consisted of sixty or so baronial families, all of whom could trace their lineage to the Battle of Hastings, although the distinction between Norman and Saxon was now so vague as to be meaningless. Then there were the knights, who had enough land and income to pay for a horse and battle armor, or a net worth of forty pounds. Underneath the knights were the esquires, a sort of proto-middle-class, followed by the yeomen, high-ranking peasants with small amounts of land.[1]

At the bottom of the pile were the unfree peasants, the 'villeins' (from the Latin *villa*, or house) or serfs, who were tied to the land and had little personal freedom. Serfdom had replaced slavery under the Normans following pressure from the Church, and although it was somewhat better (a serf could not be separated from family members or arbitrarily killed, although his lord was often in charge of the local court), it was not by any means a laugh a minute. Serfdom was widespread, so much so that in 1290 some 60 percent of the rural population were unfree and that had probably not changed that much in a century.[2] Some regions had fewer serfs, in particular Kent, which had a rising free class of peasants, and across Western Europe serfdom was in decline.

The lower classes were largely despised, reflected in the fact that numerous words come from old names for peasants, such as villain (*villein*), boor (*gabore*, a low-grade Anglo-Saxon), and churlish (*churl*). The most popular book of the late medieval period, Sir Thomas Malory's *The Death of Arthur*, features just one peasant with a speaking part, who immediately gets knocked on the head for refusing to let a knight requisition his cart. Froissart said of the English peasantry that they were 'cruel, perfidious, and disloyal . . . they will not allow them [aristocracy] to have anything—even an egg or a chicken—without paying for it.'[3]

Society was not completely static, and it was possible to rise up in the world. William of Wykeham, the chancellor of England and bishop of Winchester, was the son of a serf and went on to found New College Oxford and Winchester College, the country's first public school,[4] which still uses his personal motto: 'Manners Makyth Man.' While Clement Paston was a churl, the lowest form of life, the following century his family rose up to become near-aristocrats. But this was rare.

The peasant's life was grim. In the North, which was poorer, laborers often lived with the farmer who employed them, sleeping on hay in the barn along with livestock; in the South, they inhabited little 'tent-shaped hovels,' which was a step up, of sorts. The peasant diet was generally inadequate, dominated by poor-quality bread; meat or even fish was a rare treat, and while there was a small amount of fruit it was considered dangerous to one's health. Skeletons from the time show that malnutrition and vitamin deficiencies were commonplace.

Rural workers were also ground down by the various services they had to give their masters. On top of free labor, they had to pay the lord the *merchet*, a payment to allow a daughter to marry; *heriot*, a death duty; *leyrwite*, a fine paid mostly by women for forbidden sexual activity, which ran the risk of lowering a serf's market value if she got pregnant. There was also *chevages*, permission to leave the manor; *faldagium*, permission to graze animals outside the lord's fold; an entry fine, when taking on new land; *tallages*, a land tax; and suit of mill, which forced villeins to use the lord's mill at his price. The Church also took a tenth of everything the serfs produced, although the *tithe* was widely avoided.

The serf could not leave the manor nor send his son to school without his lord's agreement, and anyone who left his master's land to get work elsewhere could end up imprisoned, be sent to the stocks, have his back whipped or ears cropped. The upside of serfdom was that the lord was also supposed to protect the property of his tenants, and help if a family member was disabled or kidnapped or a victim of crime, but if the lord didn't feel like it, there wasn't much the serf could do.

On top of this, a serf couldn't bake bread in his own shack and had to have his corn ground at a mill run by the lord and his servant, the miller. Millers were hated because they often ripped off the peasants, which may be why the name is uncommon in England, and most Americans with the surname were originally *Muller*. If surnames were adopted today, there would not be many John Parking Meterattendant or William Divorcelawyer, for instance.

When a villein died, his lord could take his best beast, and the local priest would get the second best. Then the lord could, and often did, force his wife to remarry in order to replenish the workforce; in Brightwaltham, Berkshire, in 1335, six widows were lined up and ordered to remarry if they wished to keep their husbands' land.

Understandably, Froissart's complaint about the peasantry would probably not have met with much sympathy.

Agricultural labor was back-breaking work, but outside of harvest time most peasants were also underemployed, and there were just too many useless hands and mouths for much of the year. However, this all changed with the Plague, which disproportionately hit the poor with death rates of 50 percent among serfs compared to 27 percent among the gentry and esquires. The upside of this, if it can be seen that way, was that their market value shot up.

A plowman's wage went up from two shillings to ten shillings in 1350, and a craftsmen's income was now three times what it was in 1300. From 1360–1380, the bishop of Winchester observed that the price of wheat rose by 6 percent, but the amount he paid laborers rose by 69 percent. Some workers now even had paid holidays, free lodgings, and improved perks, with harvest laborers getting twice as much ale per day as previously and receiving bread made of wheat and not barley. This shouldn't be overplayed, as the food would have been bland or disgusting, but there was a general rise in living standards, and, by 1400, most people had better food, like white bread, beef, mutton, and fish; beer with hops was introduced from the Low Countries, replacing the fairly disgusting porridgey stuff people used to drink (despite this there was a concerted effort to ban the newfangled foreign ale).

As the price of labor surged, many people complained that they couldn't get any of their odd jobs done; MPs protested that 'out of great malice' laborers and servants leave their manors and, 'if their masters reprove them for bad service or offer to pay them according to the said statutes, they fly and run suddenly away out of their service and out of their country . . . and live wicked lives and rob the poor in simple villages in bodies of two and three together.'

The poet William Langland was astonished at the demands of workers: 'Draught-ale was not good enough for them anymore, nor bacon, but they must have fresh meat or fish, fried or baked and chaud [hot] or plus chaud at that, lest they catch a chill on their stomachs. So it is nowadays. The laborer is angry unless he gets high wages.' Langland said the peasants had become haughty about food: 'They deign not to dine on day-old vegetables . . . penny ale will not do, nor a piece of bacon' but they had to have cooked meat, the ungrateful sods.

The authorities responded to the problem by instigating hopeless laws to fix wages, although these were mostly to help small farmers and employers, not big landowners (Langland was certainly no aristocrat). The Ordinance of Laborers was issued in 1349, the aim being to set wages at pre-Plague fixed levels, forcing men and women to work for the same wages and forbidding employers to pay more on pain of imprisonment. However, most people ignored it, and peasants continued leaving their manors in large numbers to take advantage of more attractive offers elsewhere, even though this was illegal.

After the pestilence, some peasants took legal action to remove themselves from feudal ties. From 1377–1388, over forty manors in the South asked the crown to verify their entries in the Domesday Book—commissioned back in 1086 to show who owned what—to prove they were part of royal domain and so exempt from labor services. One manor succeeded in doing this by showing it belonged to Anglo-Saxon kings.

The 1349 law was followed by the Statute of Laborers in 1351, which made it illegal to demand higher wages than earned before 1348, and attacked the 'malice of servants' who 'for the sake of their own comfort and greed completely disregard the said ordinance' and demand 'outrageous wages.' Anyone who tried to charge above pre-Plague prices was given three days' imprisonment in the stocks for first offenders; a further law, in 1360, stated that fugitive laborers were to be branded with an F if they left their manor. By the 1370s, 70 percent of legal business in kings' courts involved labor legislation, which suggested it was clogging up the workings of government. The authorities even built stocks in Gloucestershire to imprison those who took higher wages but they had to pay the carpenter who built it 5½ pence a day, twice the legal limit.[5]

In 1363, Parliament even passed laws against people dressing above their station, restricting the wearing of furs and of pointed shoes, as such footwear on the lower orders was seen as unduly provocative. Under these regulations, nobles were allowed toe-extensions of up to twenty-four inches, gentlemen up to twelve inches, and merchants up to six and a half inches. All this seems rather bizarre from our perspective, yet at the time dressing as if from a different social class was considered a form of fraud. This Sumptuary Law of 1363 divided the population into seven social classes, and stated that no one below the level of gentleman could wear velvet, while no serving woman could have a veil costing more than twelve pence.[6]

In 1377, four months after Edward III died, the first poll tax went into effect, taking one thirteenth of a peasant's wage, which was entirely swallowed up by the cost of the war, the equivalent of throwing cotton wool into a furnace.

The government needed to raise fifty thousand pounds but could only manage twenty-two thousand from the second poll tax in 1379, which was fairer, but this was soon swallowed up by yet another *chevauchée*, this time by Gaunt's excitable younger brother Thomas of Woodstock. In 1380, the English crown jewels also had to be pawned to pay for Woodstock's invasion of Northern France, which turned out to be 'an open-eyed walk into privation, hunger, and ultimate futility.'[7] The aim was to support allies in Brittany, but Woodstock took a bizarre long route through Champagne and Burgundy hoping to win glory in battle, without luck—exactly the same tactics that were used last time with exactly the same result. The tax of 1379 also helped pay for an especially horrific episode the following year when Sir John Arundel led a raid in Brittany, the gang ostentatiously embarking with a wardrobe of fifty-two suits embodied in gold, an indication of how much warfare at the time was about showing off. They turned up at a convent where a wedding was being held, raped all the nuns and female wedding guests, and then kidnapped everyone, but were caught in a storm that sunk all twenty of their ships, killing one thousand men and sparing just eight. Many people considered this divine punishment, although all the female captives were also drowned, making them divine collateral damage.

There was now increasing signs of agitation across the country, including among the merchant leaders of London who were so hysterical about a supposed royal plot to move the trading capital to Southampton that a trading guild arranged the murder of the Genoan ambassador, who they believed to be implicated in the imaginary conspiracy. At York in November 1380, there were signs of growing unrest when 'various malefactors among the commons drove the mayor, John Gysburn, out of the city, smashed their way into the Guildhall with axes, seized one Simon de Quixlay, forced him to become the new mayor, and made all the members of the city council swear allegiance to him.' De Quixlay, despite becoming mayor in rather unusual circumstances, went on to win two reelections. In early 1381, the first tax collector was murdered, an Oxfordshire man with the appropriate name William Payable, set upon by persons unknown.

France also suffered further outburst of violence by agitators called the 'Tuchins,' from *tue-chiens*, or 'kill-dogs,' who, as their name suggests, were not a peaceful protest movement. It all ended in Montpelier in 1379 when the authorities put to death six hundred individuals, deciding that two hundred would be hanged, two hundred beheaded, and two hundred burned, all their property confiscated, and all their children sentenced to perpetual servitude.

The first two poll taxes had some success in raising money, but it was not enough and, in November 1380, Parliament voted for a third tax, this time to fund John of Gaunt's military adventure in Spain where he was claiming the throne, an unpopular war led by an unpopular man, and which seemed to have no benefit whatsoever for people in England. This was the spark for an uprising, which at the time was called the 'Mad Multitude' or 'Rumor,' the term 'Peasants' Revolt' only being coined several centuries later. Many historians dislike the term, since peasant in our mind has particular connotations of dull-witted yokels chewing straw and waving pitchforks, while many of the 'rustics' were what we would now call middle class in the United States or lower-middle class in England.

The new tax came during a bad harvest and tough winter, the authorities demanding payment from everyone over the age of fifteen excluding beggars. Unsurprisingly, much of the population mysteriously disappeared: 450,000 people who had paid the tax in 1377 evaded the 1381 one, and Essex, which had a taxable population of 48,000 in 1377, suddenly went down to 30,748 four years later. Essex was rich, and poorer areas like Cornwall and Lancashire 'lost' more than half their population. In the spring of 1381, commissioners were sent into Essex demanding that £66,666 be paid by April 21, with sergeants at arms assigned to travel with commissions, who were basically heavily armed tough guys hired by the authorities to intimidate the locals.

It was rumored that in the village of Fobbing a commissioner 'shamelessly lifted the young girls' skirts' to test whether they had pubic hair, which would make them adults and so liable to taxation. It was also believed that the daughter of Thomas Baker, the leader of the first rebel company in Essex, had been molested by tax inspectors. Whether any of this was true or it was just ale-fueled medieval whispering, we can't tell. Whatever the initial spark, violence erupted in three villages, Fobbing, Corringham, and Stanford-le-Hope, with angry rustics raiding the home of a local official, where they beheaded two clerks and drank three barrels of wine. They were now heavily armed with rusty swords, axes, and bows, and drunk—drunk on power, but also just drunk. Soon the Essex rebels were seen walking around the county with three poles, each with a head on it. (Since the reign of Edward I the authorities had tried to keep the population war ready, so the possession of dangerous weapons was not just permitted but encouraged and sometimes enforced.) The violence soon spread across the Thames Estuary to Kent where a leader emerged in the form of Wat Tyler.[8] Right from the start, the rebels used violence and coercion to get people to join the uprising, and almost anyone who held a position of authority was at risk of being attacked as the mob swept through. They 'went to the manors and townships of those who would not rise with them, and cast their houses to the ground or set fire to them.' The abbeys and monasteries were especially targeted because they were the last to abolish serfdom and allowed peasants to work as free labor. There was also a fair amount of organization from the beginning; anyone within twelve leagues of the sea was instructed to remain in their village in case the French invaded. They claimed to be patriots and to be loyal to the king and 'the true commons.'

Thomas Walsingham, a hostile observer, said 'those who refused or disdained to' join in 'would know that they would have their possessions pillaged, their homes burned down or demolished, and themselves be executed.' Froissart, not hugely sympathetic to the plight of the working class anywhere, said that 'England was at a point to have been lost beyond recovery,' but 'three fourths of these people could not tell what to ask or demand but followed each other like beasts.' That's probably true of most protests, to be fair.

Rebels in Kent attacked prisons and released the inmates, among them a cleric called John Ball, who had been well-known to the authorities for twenty years. Ball had had been imprisoned three times by the archbishop of Canterbury and was well-known as an irritant, preaching against inequality and corruption and attacking the Church hierarchy. The archbishop of Canterbury accused Ball of preaching sermons that 'reeked of heretical depravity,' while Walsingham criticized a speech of Ball's in which he called for 'equality of liberty and nobility, as well as of dignity and power' as 'perverse . . . insane . . . ravings.'

Today he'd be a regular on BBC radio or NPR talking about social justice, but the authorities had less time for lefty vicars back then, and he'd spent much of his in jail. John Ball coined the famous ditty 'when Adam delved and Eve span, and who was then the gentleman,' to justify his radical vision of equality, and looked forward to a time of 'lechery without shame' and 'gluttony without blame,' which all sounds very 1960s.

Ball, Wat Tyler, and a third man, Jack Straw, are the only three leaders who are widely remembered, even though the actual records don't say much about Tyler and almost nothing about Straw; as with much of history, the difference between fame and total nonentity is minimal.

The rebels marched on London, fifty thousand of them according to Froissart, but probably closer to ten thousand; at any rate, a frightening mob which, in terms of men of fighting age, outnumbered Londoners. 'Death to all lawyers. John Ball hath rungeth your bell' the crowds shouted, and in Kent the peasants destroyed all lawyers' homes on their way to the capital; they really hated lawyers, although everyone at the time did.

Within London itself there was huge anger among the merchants, especially toward Gaunt, who luckily for him was away on the Scottish border. This meant that there was a total absence of leadership in London, and the king was now at the age when most boys are concerned with spots and first crushes, rather than placating angry rural mobs.

The Kentishmen reached the edge of London on June 12, assembling at Blackheath, southeast of the city where the king came to meet them by boat. The rebels made a list of demands to the monarch, which were largely ridiculous, including the execution of most of his advisors, some of whom were actually with him at the time and so—presumably—would have advised against it. Among the fifteen men of which they wanted the heads was Chief Justice Sir Robert Belknap, so hated that at Richard II's coronation the citizens erected a likeness of his head on a water conduit along the route of the parade, 'so that all who passed would see him spewing wine out of his ridiculous mouth.' Also on the list was John of Gaunt, the archbishop of Canterbury, the head of the exchequer, and basically everyone in power except the king who, in Tyler's fantasy world, would rule alongside Tyler.[9] Some historians, however, suggest that the pubescent ruler was quite sympathetic to the idea of having all his elders beheaded, as many fourteen-year-olds would be.

Soon, the mob were in Southwark, on the other side of London Bridge, and then the fateful decision was made to allow them to cross, and destruction ensued, much of it clearly assisted by Londoners.

The mob's first target was Gaunt's Savoy Palace, to the west of the city, which he had inherited from his father-in-law Henry of Lancaster, and, as rumor of the mob spread, its staff scurried away with whatever they could grab. The palace was very sumptuous, with a front door looking out onto the Strand, the road from London to Westminster, and a back door with its own jetty on the Thames. Hugely expensive, it had been built by Lancaster at the cost of thirty-five thousand pounds, the equivalent of four and a half month's wages for an entire English army. Funded by mindless English violence in France, it was destroyed in the same manner, and when the rebels arrived, everything was thrown into a fire in the hall, including huge amounts of gold and silver. One headboard they destroyed was worth one thousand marks, roughly equivalent to $650,000 today. Despite all this wanton destruction, the riot leaders banned anyone from stealing; one man was caught trying to take a silver goblet from the duke's wardrobe and was hurled into the flames.

At some point, a barrel they thought was gold or silver was thrown in the fire; unfortunately, it turned out to be gunpowder and caused a huge explosion, causing a section of the building to collapse. Thirty of the rioters who had discovered the wine cellars, where they had been getting drunk and having—until then—a wonderful time, were trapped in the burning building; it took over a week for them to die and no one came to help them.

It was now decided to have another meeting with the rebels, this time to the east of the city at Mile End, which turned out to be even more disastrous. By this stage, the uprising had evolved into something even worse, and the throng the king met was considerably more disreputable than at Blackheath. The original mob was now joined by random farmhands from around the southeast of England; they also took to fighting among themselves, and a Kent man was stabbed to death near Mile End by another rustic after an argument broke out.

However, now the peasants made quite reasonable demands, basically an end to serfdom and a limit on rent of 4 pence per acre, but also that no man must be forced to work except through a contract, a program that was not totally impossible to imagine.

Richard agreed to everything, but blundered by going further and saying that the peasants were also free to go around catching 'traitors' and bring them to him. This was a terrible mistake, which was interpreted as being a carte blanche to attack anyone they decreed to be traitors, which to an angry mob can be quite a loose definition. Whatever restraint had existed now disappeared.

Most of the leading figures were at this point cowering in the Tower of London, but they could not hold out any longer and the order was given for the rustics to enter. The mob found Simon Sudbury, the archbishop of Canterbury, who was at prayer, and Thomas Walsingham writes, 'those limbs of Satan laid their impious hands on him and tore him from the Chapel.' They chased him through the Great Hall and Royal Wardrobe, stealing everything in the kitchens, bedchambers, and armory; in the queen mother's room, they smashed up the furniture and cut up her bedclothes. The rustics humiliated Queen Joan by forcing her to kiss rioters, after which she passed out with shock; however, in the confusion she was led out to a boat that took her away.

Others were not so lucky, among them the Lord Treasurer Robert Hales, John of Gaunt's doctor, leading financier Sir Richard Lyons, and John Legge, who had had the bright idea of the poll tax in the first place. They were all decapitated, their heads stuck on pikes and paraded around the city. Archbishop Sudbury had almost escaped, but was spotted by a 'wicked woman' and was killed with eight blows in a highly amateurish way; after the second fell he was still alive enough to touch the wound.

The king's fourteen-year-old cousin Henry of Derby, the son of Gaunt, was among those who cowered in the Tower; he would almost certainly have been murdered but one of the rioters, a soldier called John Ferrour who had also helped destroy the Savoy Palace, took pity on the boy and saved his life by hiding him.

Now the violence exploded, with various scores being settled. A fishmonger called Sir Robert Allen got some Kent rebels to attack a rival; a mob almost burned down Guildhall because a brewer called Walter ate Keye was trying to find a document called the Jubilee Book, which supposedly listed debts. Among the targets was Richard Imworth, keeper of the King's Bench prison in Southwark, described as a 'tormentor without pity,' although such a job at the time did not exactly attract people persons. Imworth hid by the shrine of Edward the Confessor, hoping that this might put them off, but it made no difference. The mob even killed a valet called John of Greenfield because he was overheard 'speaking well of John of Gaunt's murdered physician William Appleton and other victims of the rebels' murderous purges.'

On London Bridge, they burned down a brothel owned by the lord mayor, and a spokesman for the peasants swore to kill 'all lawyers and servants of the King they could find.' They rounded on foreigners, killing thirty-five Flemish traders who lived in the city in perhaps the most brutal event of the whole uprising. Flemings were identified by being asked to say 'brede and chees'; pronunciation tests were a common way of marking foreigners in massacres dating back to the Bible when the Ephraimites were identified by the Gileadites because they could not say the Hebrew word 'shibboleth.' In 1272, during 'the Sicilian Vespers,' the French were found out by their inability to say the Sicilian word *ciciri*, while in the Lebanese civil war of 1975–1990, Christian militiamen would present tomatoes to suspected Palestinians and ask what they were.

The rioters destroyed any documents they could find to remove evidence of serfdom. According to the *Historia Anglicana*: 'they strove to burn all old records; and they butchered anyone who might know or be able to commit to memory the contents of old or new documents. It was dangerous enough to be known as a clerk, but especially dangerous if an ink-pot should be found at one's elbow; such men scarcely or ever escaped from the hands of the rebels.'

Thomas Walsingham said 'the rebels committed . . . many other enormities without sparing any grade or order—in churches and cemeteries, in roads and streets as well as in houses and fields . . . After a whole day spent in such detestable actions, they were at last exhausted by their labors and the drinking of so much more wine than usual; thus in the evening you could see them lying scattered about on the streets and under the walls, sleeping like slaughtered pigs.' The best that can be said about the rioters is that they were restrained compared to the Jacquerie, which was far more gruesome.

There were now risings across the eastern counties of Hertfordshire, Cambridgeshire, Norfolk, and Suffolk, with various renegades running around the countryside.[10] In Bury St. Edmunds, a mob under the leadership of a disgruntled priest called John Wrawe hunted down all the lawyers and clerics. In nearby Cambridge, the townies forced the scholars to renounce their privileges under pain of death; at what is now Queen's College, the mob ransacked the library, killed the university chancellor, and burned all the books in the town square, a local woman shouting 'away with the learning of the clerks.' The urban elite fully supported the rebels, having always hated everyone involved in the university, and even the mayor took part.[11]

Wrawe went around the area between Cambridge, Bury, and Ely on a rampage of extortion, arson, robbery, and murder. His gang beheaded Sir John Cavendish, chief justice of the King's Bench, in the village of Lakenheath, and his head was displayed on the pillory in the marketplace at Bury, along with John of Cambridge, the local prior. The two heads were put on sticks and were made to kiss in some bizarre puppet show that all the villagers found amusing.

On top of economic distress, there was a romantic, nationalistic aspect to the uprising, with many peasants inspired by a noble vision of a return to Anglo-Saxon times when all were free and equal, an egalitarian golden age that entirely existed in their imaginations. There has always been a tradition that England was free and even progressive before the Norman invasion of 1066 led to a division between 'us and them,' which slightly ignores the fact that up to a quarter of adults at the time were slaves, and for the most part life as an Anglo-Saxon peasant was horrific.

However, the rustics had it in their heads that the Church had hidden away secret proof of older, fairer laws, which they called the Law of Winchester after the old capital of Wessex.[12] These had the attractive combinations of being both egalitarian and absurdly authoritarian; they apparently called on all villagers to share in keeping the peace and 'sanctioned unsparing punishment for all criminals.' In the words of the law, 'no one will be spared and no felony will be concealed,' the sort of no-nonsense platform that appealed to a fourteenth-century villager.

In St. Alban's, just north of London, the rebels attacked the abbey under the belief that the abbot had a charter granted by King Offa in the eighth century in which all 'their ancient liberties and rights were written down in beautiful letters of gold and azure.' They demanded that the monks hand over documentary proof of the Law of Winchester, having already helpfully burned all the abbey's legal charters in a big bonfire.

Despite having no evidence of this charter or that it had ever existed, the rebels gave the monks an ultimatum on Saturday to produce Offa's document the following week, and nothing they said could persuade the mob it did not exist. By the Sunday morning, the monks were panicking and their leader did not know what to do: 'But faced by the rebels' demands for physical proofs of their mystic traditions, he was as helpless as if they had asked him to saddle them a unicorn.'[13]

The monks were now preparing to flee, and the crowd was swollen by men from nearby villages such as Watford, Luton, Barnet, and Rickmansworth. They were saved only by a rumor about what had happened in London and the dreadful fate of Wat Tyler, which for once turned out to be true. Most of the rustics drifted away, and those who stayed began to behave themselves.

Back in the city, the rebels had by now demanded an end to all lordship, which for the fourteenth century was just silly. Under their scheme there would be no bishop except one prelate, the archbishop of Canterbury (funnily enough, there was now a vacancy), while all clerical lands and possessions except bare essentials would be divided among people of the parish. Wat Tyler, the rebellion's de facto leader, boasted that 'in four days' time all the laws of England would be issuing from his mouth.'

King Richard agreed to meet the rebel leader at Smithfield, outside the city. Tyler, a common laborer from Dartford,[14] approached and showed great disrespect by raising his hands to the monarch—rude even today but unthinkable back then, especially in an age when men were routinely armed. Tyler also insulted the king by drinking from a jug of water in a deliberately coarse way and spat in front of him. Using intrusive body language, Tyler moved so close that his 'horse's tail [was] under the very nose of the king's horse.'

The Kentishman made a series of demands, including the redistribution of Church lands to the poor, and for 'all men to be one condition'; he might as well have demanded a million dollars in cash and a plane to Cuba, such was the likelihood of a fourteenth-century feudal monarch instigating reforms Left-wing even for the standards of today.

The peasant leader then ordered beers all around, but when one of the king's men muttered that he was 'the biggest thief in Kent,' Tyler drew his knife. Fearing for the monarch, Mayor William Walworth—a former fishmonger—pulled out his own weapon, a short dagger; Tyler stabbed Walworth first but he had body armor on and stabbed back, calling Tyler 'a stinking wretch.'[15] Walworth was left to die on the ground—but then, people who slurp when they drink are annoying.

The mob seemed so stunned by what was going on that they couldn't even get angry. Richard held his nerve and ordered them to follow him to Smithfield, saying he was their 'captain.' In the meantime, the authorities had finally got around to arming a body of Londoners prepared to put down the rioters with what modern military types call 'extreme prejudice,' who were amassed and sent to Smithfield. Now surrounded by armed men, the rebels lost their nerve and suddenly weren't in the mood to make radical demands, instead begging for mercy and asking to go home. The king placated the mob and offered safe passage and an end to the poll tax; the rebels, for some reason, were still convinced the king was on their side.

Tyler had been fatally wounded and taken to St. Bart's hospital nearby. Just to make sure, Walworth went there and had him dragged from his deathbed bleeding, propped up in a field, and beheaded.

Meanwhile, in East Anglia, the uprising was dealt with by Bishop Despenser of Norwich, a man of the cloth who was rather unorthodox in his interests. The grandson of Edward II's crony, Despenser had in his youth been one of the pope's military commanders, and how he ended up in the Church is something of a mystery. He mustered a group of armed men, some archers and horsemen, and headed to Peterborough, where he went into battle like 'a wild boar gnashing his teeth, sparing neither himself nor his enemies.'[16] The rebels hid inside a church but, ignoring the rules of sanctuary, the bishop massacred them all, personally executing the ringleader.

The ever-hard-line Henry Knighton, quoting St. John the Evangelist, spoke approvingly of Despenser's actions: 'You will rule them with iron rods and break them like a potter's vessel.'

Now, with the rebels on the back foot, the counterterror began. In Essex, the king gave them a moving speech in which he said: 'You wretches, detestable on land and sea; you who seek equality with lords are unworthy to live. Give this message to your colleagues. Rustics you were and rustics you are still; you will remain in bondage not as before but incomparably harsher. For as long as you live we will strive to suppress you, and your misery will be an example in the eyes of posterity.' Well, this is how Walsingham reported him, but it conflicts with evidence that the king was still suggesting mercy late into the year when most MPs were demanding blood.

Richard called on loyal yeomen around the southeast to help him, raising as many as forty thousand volunteers for the brutal crackdown; hundreds of the rebels were massacred as they made their way back to the Home Counties. John Ball was arrested in Coventry and executed in front of the king; Walworth, for his good work, was knighted.

Between July and September 1381, anywhere between fifteen hundred and seven thousand people were killed by the authorities in retribution; in Cambridgeshire John Shirley, a Nottinghamshire man, was heard saying that John Ball was a 'true and worthy man,' and was immediately strung up. Such was the reaction that William Courtenay, the new and understandably hard-line archbishop of Canterbury, even made six of his serfs publicly parade around the church carrying straw because they had delivered hay and straw to him in secret to avoid being seen doing it in public; in the future, serfs were expected to revel in their serfdom.

Despite this disaster, the poll tax was attempted again in 1497 and led to another rebellion. Luckily they never tried it again![17]

The tax, however, was a useful record for historians, and one of the interesting things it recorded was how unimaginative people were with names they gave their children. The returns from Sheffield showed that 33 percent of men were called John and 19 percent William, and this was not unusual. It also recorded some funny medieval surnames for posterity, which otherwise would have been lost, among them William Catface, William Two yer old, Margaret Tenwynter, Henry Neverafered, and William Standupryght.[18]

Although serfdom largely died out in the following century, the rebellion probably didn't help and rather led to an authoritarian response and a hardening of attitudes toward the peasants. There followed many spiteful laws, with the House of Commons even trying to ban villeins from sending their children to school—the king vetoed it. In 1390, a Parliament full of landholders passed a law for one year's imprisonment for every layman not possessing landed property worth forty shillings a year 'who should presume to keep hunting-dogs or use ferrets or snares to catch deer, hares, rabbits, or any other game.' Hunting, they said, 'was the sport of gentlefolk' while anti-poaching laws became more fierce.

Serfdom fell out of use anyway for economic reasons, although personal bondage didn't entirely end in the fourteenth century. The *merchet, heriot,* and *chevage* remained for much longer, and the last legal reference to a bondsman was made in 1586 in a legal dispute, while 'manorial incidents lingered to irritate tenants sometimes even in the nineteenth century.' Such feudal dues were only formally abolished in 1922.[19]

CHAPTER TEN

Schism

John Ball was a Lollard, a heresy founded by Yorkshire-born theologian John Wycliffe in the gloomy post-Plague mood, a time when many people turned against the religious authorities.

The Church had been badly damaged by the Black Death, with as many as two-thirds of clerics in some areas killed off, largely because they had to tend to the sick.[1] (Also hit hard were doctors; in Perpignan, only one out of eight physicians survived.) The number of people in holy orders at Rievaulx, a Cistercian abbey in Yorkshire, went from four hundred to just eighteen by 1381, although this was accelerated by a general decline in monk numbers. Wothorpe Priory in Northamptonshire had just one surviving nun after the disease and had to be dissolved; it was not the only institution that suffered this fate.

Although clergymen were disproportionately hit by the Plague, not everyone was too sad about this. The miserable Knighton wrote, 'Of the English Austin Friars at Avignon not one remained, nor did men care' and that 'at Marseilles, of one hundred and fifty Franciscans, not one survived to tell the tale; and a good job too!' He added that only seven friars survived out of 160 at Maguelonne 'and that was enough.' Knighton further claimed that no one noticed that sixty-six Carmelites at Avignon had died of the Plague because everyone 'thought that these friars had killed each other,' which seems pretty unlikely.

After the Black Death, people were so desperate for priests that almost anyone could get the job, and, in 1349, the Church also decreed that anyone could perform the last rites, even women. Inevitably, as in any area where people found they could do things for themselves, it made them unwilling to pay a professional to do it.

Although many priests had died, there was also anger at how others had (understandably) fled rather than carry out their job of deathbed companions to spluttering, rancid Plague victims. There was also discontent at the luxurious lives priests supposedly led, and although it is a contentious subject that gets lost in later sectarian controversy, there is some evidence of monks enjoying the good life; forensic archaeology suggests that alcohol accounted for 19 percent of their daily calorie intake, compared to an average of 5 percent today, and some consumed upwards of seven thousand calories per day.[2]

Certainly, corruption was in the Vatican, especially in the appointment of jobs: the sons of aristocrats were often made archbishops at eighteen, and in Bohemia in the early fourteenth century, a boy of seven was appointed to a lucrative parish. There was also the blatant use of money to buy off Church dispensations—with fixed prices to legitimize children or marry cousins, or to trade with Muslims, all supposedly banned—with the money collected and counted by Italian bankers inside the papal palace.

With the world shook up, more uncertain, and violent, the Plague had led to an ugly anticlerical mood across Europe. In Germany in 1372, papal tax collectors were 'seized, mutilated, imprisoned, some even strangled' after Pope Gregory XI demanded a new tithe, something many clerics refused to pay. Some priests in that country were so short of money they left their jobs or supplemented their income by working in taverns.

There was a noted upturn in violence against churchmen in England, too. In December 1349, Bishop Ralph of Shrewsbury was attacked in Yeovil by some 'sons of perdition' armed with 'bows, arrows, iron bars, and other kinds of arms.' This siege went on all night until they were rescued the following day by 'devout sons of the Church' who overpowered the sixty miscreants. The citizens of Worcester that same year had broken down the gates of the Priory of St. Marcy and attacked the monks with bows and arrows and tried to set fire to the building.

It was in this atmosphere that Lollardy arose. There had been heresies before: in 1166, some twenty heretics who denied Mass and the sacrament of baptism turned up in England. They were branded and left to die in the cold. But England had never seen anything like the Cathars, the ultra-austere group from the south of France who believed all matter to be essentially evil.

Wycliffe, an Oxford academic, criticized the power and corruption of the clergy believing that any pious man could have the same religious power as a priest, and that the Church hierarchy alone did not hold the answer to peoples' salvation. Arguing that the common people should be able to read the Bible for themselves, and not take their priests' word for it, Wycliffe became at first a nuisance and then dangerous. His followers became known as Lollards, from *loller*, a Dutch word for itinerant preachers; it also meant 'mumbler,' as they were known to mutter memorized passages of the Bible. Most Lollards lived within sixty miles of London, the heresy being concentrated in the same areas that would become Protestant a century and a half later.

Wycliffe's main argument to start with was that the Church had too much money, and had become overly concerned with material wealth. In 1410, it was calculated that selling off Church property in England could fund the creation of fifteen earls, fifteen hundred knights, sixty-two hundred esquires, one hundred almshouses, fifteen universities, and fifteen thousand priests, *and* still leave change.

His idea of taking wealth from the Church was popular with some aristocrats who supported Wycliffe out of greed more than anything else. In particular, he received the protection of John of Gaunt, who brought Wycliffe to London in 1376 to preach in favor of increasing Crown revenues by taxing Church wealth.

However, many of his sympathizers were scared away in 1379 when Wycliffe attacked transubstantiation, the Catholic doctrine that Communion bread literally turns into the body of Christ during Mass. This was seriously heretical. His enemies called him 'Wicked Life,' which sounds rather feeble as an insult; when he attacked papal authority on top of this he was denounced as 'the Great Heresiarch.'

The uprising of 1381 further frightened richer supporters, even though it wasn't actually inspired by Lollardy, but because it tapped into the same pool of anger against the authorities. Then, in 1382, Wycliffe produced something that hadn't been done for some time—an English Bible. Translating the holy book into the language of the people was not illegal in itself, and there were older English versions, but the Church wished to have control over it; like any religious text, it can be interpreted in a number of ways justifying just about any moral or political stance the believer wants to see, and this can lead to dangerous and literal interpretations. There were also a lot of bad translations by enthusiastic amateurs—the early English Bibles stated that Jesus had turned water into cider, which doesn't have quite the same magic to it, especially as cider in England is traditionally drunk by people who speak in pirate-like ooh-aarrgh regional accents and don't have a full set of teeth.

The Church was a very powerful enemy, controlling not just men's souls, but schools and hospitals, the welfare of the poor, and even mental asylums. Bethlehem—shortened to Bedlam—hospital in Bishopsgate, London, had been established in 1377, and local people would while away Sunday afternoons by going there to laugh at the lunatics. For a penny you could look into their cells, and even poke them with sticks—one Tuesday a month was free—which must have helped the patients' mental health to no end.

Wycliffe died peacefully in 1384. However, the Lollards were damned as heretics and, in 1401, burning at the stake was introduced for the first time for anyone who denied transubstantiation, heralding two centuries of increasing religious intolerance and fanaticism. Wycliffe's bones were even dug up in 1415 and burned, the same year that Bohemian heretic Jan Hus also was burned (unfortunately for him, while still alive). Hus had led a movement in the modern-day Czech Republic called the Hussites, who—after an uprising that saw the first effective use of firearms—were squashed by the Church. Hus's ashes were chucked in a river on the order of the pope.

It did not help that during this time the Catholic Church seemed to be having a sort of collective nervous breakdown called the Schism: from the 1370s, there were two separate popes who mutually excommunicated each other and were in a state of extreme hostility. One was a mass murderer; the other was totally insane.

In 1378, Pope Gregory XI had died, and a replacement was chosen among 'scenes of mob violence and intimidation' in Rome.[3] The people's choice, local man Bartolomeo Prignano, was a fresh face who had no previous experience as a cardinal, but there was a movement to have someone outside of the hierarchy who was not a career churchman.

The new pope, named Urban VI, proved to be a revelation, but in a bad way. Urban, it increasingly transpired, was mentally unbalanced at best, if not entirely insane, the job promotion having set off something in his brain. As Barbara Tuchman wrote, 'From a humble unspectacular official totally unprepared for the papal throne, he was transformed overnight into an implacable scourge of simony, moved less by religious zeal than by simple hatred and jealousy of privilege.' He attacked cardinals for 'absenteeism, luxury, and lascivious life' and 'berated them without tact or dignity, his face growing purple and his voice hoarse with rage. He interrupted them with rude invective and cries of "Rubbish!" and "Shut your mouth!"'

When bishops came to pay homage to him he said they'd deserted their flock; when given money owed the Holy See he said to his treasurer 'to keep thy money to thyself, to perish with thee.' He called one cardinal a half-wit and tried to punch another, but was physically restrained; he also publicly accused a cardinal of corruption, which may have been true, but you don't *say* it.

Popes were supposed to stay out of secular politics, when appropriate, but Urban then announced that the Kingdom of Naples was badly governed because the ruler, Queen Joanna, was a woman and he threatened to put her in a nunnery. Soon, some cardinals (mostly French) declared Urban's election invalid on the grounds it had been done while they were in 'fear of their lives' to the sound of 'tumultuous and horrible voices' in Rome. In a manifesto, the rebel churchmen declared Urban to be an 'Antichrist, devil, apostate, tyrant, deceiver' who had been elected by force, and fled to France, leading to a great schism in which one pope ruled from Rome and another from Avignon.

However, their choice of 'anti-pope' was even stranger. Back in 1377, there had taken place one of the most notorious incidents of the era, the Cesena massacre. At the time, the mercenary John Hawkwood was under contract to a French cardinal, Roberto of Cambrai, when people in the city of Cesena killed some of Roberto's soldiers during one of Italy's numerous inter-city squabbles (this one with the poetic name 'The War of the Eight Saints'). Cardinal Roberto offered the citizens amnesty if they surrendered their arms, which they did; he then summoned Hawkwood from nearby Faenza, where he was busy engaging in various atrocities, and ordered him to kill everyone in Cesena.

Even Sir John said this was going a bit far, but Cardinal Roberto demanded 'blood and more blood,' and as many as eight thousand were killed and another sixteen thousand fled, with the river having turned red and the victims, including twenty-four friars, murdered in front of the main altar of their church along with their congregation. Hawkwood was slightly horrified by the whole thing and sent one thousand women out to safety in Rimini.[4] So when the dissident cardinals came to Avignon for the election, they chose, of all people, Cardinal Roberto, who had funded his campaign with money he acquired from a bishopric in Durham he had never even visited, the kind of corruption that angered Lollards. The Butcher of Cesena took the wildly inappropriate name Clement and the schism split western Christendom for decades.

Urban became ever more unpopular, and there was soon a plot to put him in protective custody, but he learned of it and arrested the six cardinals involved; as they were being tortured, he was seen outside their cell reading out liturgical texts while listening to their screams. Five of the cardinals were executed and the sixth, who was English, was spared through the intercession of Richard II.

It led to a lot of confusion, for every Christian was condemned to damnation by at least one pope, and in some regions double bishops were appointed, each proclaiming everything the other did a sacrilege. In Flanders, where the rulers sided with Clement, some Urbanists left their homes to move to another diocese. The monk of St Denis lamented the Church was pushed around 'like a prostitute found at the scene of a debauch,' and one popular saying reckoned that 'no one since the beginning of the schism had entered Paradise.'

The post-Plague period seemed to be filled with religious fanatics, such as Margery Kempe of Norfolk, a former brewer and corn grinder who became a mystic and 'professional hysteric.' She wore gold threads on her head and slashed cloaks to show her faith. She would irritate fellow pilgrims with her loud weeping on behalf of Jesus. 'Show her a crucifix and she would faint; and if she thought she was in the presence of God she would start to scream uncontrollably. She wept in public. She wept through sermons. She wept at meals—loudly and incessantly.'[5] After she met the archbishop of

York, he gave his staff five shillings 'to get her as far away from him as possible.'

In France, the religious frenzy produced men such as Pierre de Luxembourg, who 'renounced the flesh' at the age of six and forced his twelve-year-old sister to do the same. He once 'reproached his brother for laughing, on the grounds that the Gospel recorded that Jesus had wept but not laughed.' At eight he went to study in Paris where he would 'practice fasting and self-flagellation' and demanded to enter the Celestin Order, who were fashionable because they were extremely austere. Pierre was considered too young. So he would break into the order's monastery so he could lie on the ground fully clothed ready for prayers at midnight. A canon at nine, he became a bishop at fifteen and cardinal at sixteen, and his life was 'nothing but humility,' mostly spent in solitary prayer or at writing down his sins in a notebook and confessing them twice a day. Occasionally, his chaplain would feign sleep when Pierre came knocking at his door in the middle of the night to confess. The poor man died of 'consumption and self-imposed rigors' in 1387, still in his teens, and was buried in the paupers cemetery at his own request; afterwards, almost eighteen hundred miracles were attributed to him.

In 1383, Urban VI organized a Crusade against his rival, which caused chaos across Europe. As France had recognized Clement, England sided with his enemy, and so Bishop Henry Despenser led a 'Crusade' in France, which ended in disaster. He landed at Calais in April with two thousand men, but half of his force of five thousand men refused to follow the 'young, unbridled, and insolent' churchman any further, so he went home, the event described as 'the most disgraceful ever issued out of England.' It was the last English invasion of the century.[6]

CHAPTER ELEVEN

This Other Eden

Meanwhile war continued, on and off, even though people had almost forgotten what had started it. There was division in the court between the peace party, led by the young king, and the war party, led by his uncle Thomas of Woodstock. Richard did not like conflict because it meant having to share power with Parliament in order to raise money, and he was by the standards of the day quite soft. Woodstock and company were against peace because they were 'inclined to war such as had been their livelihood'; in other words, they weren't good at anything else.

France also had a new king from 1380, the twelve-year-old Charles VI, and six years later he was talked into launching the largest invasion of Britain ever. An enormous French army had gathered around Sluys; the men were ready to 'avenge ourselves for our fathers and mothers and friends whom they have killed.'

In April 1386, the French made preparations for their big armada across the Channel, and Charles VI's uncle, the Duke of Burgundy, told him 'you are the greatest King living with the greatest number of subjects' and that they will 'make this great enterprise one of eternal memory.' It was supposed to be the greatest invasion 'since God created the world.' The fact that no one has ever heard of it points to how well it went.

The people of London, 'as though maddened by wine,' went into panic mode, demolishing suburbs to prepare defenses and spending all their money madly on the assumption the French would steal everything anyway. An army was raised but the troops weren't paid so they went around looting and robbing, doing more damage to London than any French soldiers did. The English authorities could not allow northern troops to come down to defend the South as they could not be trusted.

The French plan was for an enormous army consisting of forty thousand knights and squires, sixty thousand foot soldiers, and fifty thousand horses—even if this was exaggerated, it's safe to say it was big. Some twelve hundred ships were bought for the adventure, along with two hundred thousand arrows, one thousand pounds of gunpowder, 138 stone cannonballs, five hundred ramming prows for ships, and flamethrowers. In terms of size, it dwarfed the invasion force of 1066.

'Yours will be the land of England' sung Eustache Deschamps, the French court poet who was so odd looking he was known as the 'King of Ugliness' and was said to have the skin of a boar and face of a monkey. 'Where once there was a Norman conquest, Valiant heart will make war once again.'

However, the invasion could not start before the king's uncle, the Duke of Berry, arrived and he had so far failed to show. The duke was the epitome of aristocratic decadence and far less interested in war than art, on which he spent vast amounts including one piece showing him chatting to St. Peter as he walked straight into heaven. The art was stored at his nineteen homes—two Paris town houses and seventeen castles—along with clocks, coins, mosaics, illuminated books, musical instruments, jeweled crosses, and relics. Among the relics he owned were some of Charlemagne's teeth, a bit of Elijah's cape, something that was allegedly Christ's cup from the Last Supper, a drop of the Virgin's milk as well as some of her hair and teeth, soil from various places mentioned in the Bible, the molar tooth of a giant, and gold vestments. Lots and lots of vestments. Berry ate strawberries with crystal picks mounted in silver and gold, read by candlelight from six carved ivory candleholders, and owned fifteen hundred dogs. He was a lover, not a fighter, and as for women, he once said, 'the more the merrier, but never tell the truth.'

The duke finally arrived at the invasion port of Scheldt on October 14, by which point the days were getting shorter and colder and the English Channel—which is atrocious in winter—was becoming too rough. Meanwhile, seventy-two ships loaded on a portable city were on their way from Rouen to Scheldt when they were attacked by an English fleet and three were captured.

The monk of St. Denis, who was there to give spiritual encouragement to the enterprise, now talked of bad omens; the day after Berry arrived there was terrible weather and raised waves 'like mountains' that destroyed ships. In November, the captains of 150 ships declared that the invasion was now impossible and it was all called off. Berry was widely blamed.

The decadent duke was later almost poisoned by the scheming aristocrat Charles the Bad, who after this last episode of mischief died in 'horrid circumstances' himself, aged fifty-six; he was wrapped in cloths soaked in brandy to deal with a fever, and one night a valet who was leaning over him while carrying a candle accidentally set fire to him. He took two weeks to die.

Court politics were not much better in England, where the young king was driven half-mad by the machinations of his leading lords, his paranoia eventually becoming self-fulfilling. King Richard had been born in Gascony while his father was its deeply unpopular ruler, and, after coming to England at an early age, he was taken to live at the palace at Kennington. He had a lonely childhood and grew to trust only a handful of favorites, among them his two much older half brothers, John and Thomas Holland, and another more senior man, Robert De Vere, the Earl of Oxford. De Vere dominated the king, so that 'if he had said black was white, Richard would not have contradicted him . . . By him everything was done and without him nothing done.' The relationship may have been sexual, and one hostile chronicler said that Richard liked to spend the evening with friends indulged in 'unmentionable' ways, whatever that means; but it is more likely that the art-loving and delicate king just had nothing in common with his athletic and slightly brainless relatives.

Richard II made peace with France in 1384, but was forced to invade Scotland the following year, only because it was what kings were expected to do; however, his enemies were desperate to restart the conflict and thought the king effeminate. Richard also liked dressing up, and his favorite item was a costume of white satin with cockleshells and mussel shells plated in silver. Walsingham said of Richard II that 'the king surrounds himself with "Knights of Venus" more valiant in the bedchamber than on the battlefield.' This may have been true, although such complaints of courtly decadence are found throughout history, even during the Norman period, and they really were fighters rather than lovers.

Richard was in some ways ahead of his time. His greatest influence, and friend, was his tutor Sir Simon Burley, a connection of Richard's mother who would become a father figure for an otherwise isolated young boy. Among the books that Sir Simon gave his young charge was *De Regimini Principum* by the thirteenth-century archbishop Giles of Rome, which told of a new idea: that of the divine right of kings, which had an unfortunately powerful effect on the young boy.

'A highly strung, sexless, self-obsessed exquisite with a very lofty idea of his dignity, King Richard was not exactly gifted with charm,' as one historian put it,[1] and he had an 'immature and self-centered personality.'[2] Tall, at six foot, with a sharp nose and round face, he went red and stammered when excited, and he also had the family temper—he once drew a sword on the archbishop of Canterbury and almost killed him.

As he got older, Richard began to act in a way more suited to an especially expensive film star. The king had delicate tastes, and took to carrying a handkerchief (the first known Englishman to do so). His purple tunics with monogrammed Rs also added to the decadent aristocrat look. The first king to use the royal 'we,' Richard demanded to be known not as 'my lord,' as monarchs always had until then, but 'highness,' 'majesty,' 'your high royal majesty,' and even 'most high and puissant prince.'

All Richard's subjects, however mighty, were prohibited from making eye contact, and had to kneel before him three times upon meeting the royal presence (although this was nothing like the full 'kowtow' in China, whereby anyone approaching the emperor had to kneel three times and knock his head on the floor nine times in the presence of his majesty). Later in his reign, King Richard would sit in silence on his throne for hours on end, his crown upon his head, each person in the room forced to bend their knee whenever he looked their way. Unsurprisingly people began to think he was a bit mad.

In fairness, he was just following the political fashion of the time, just as his introduction of the spoon to England followed courtly styles (people previously ate with their hands). Western Europe was moving away from the violent medieval world of baronial conflict and toward a more civilized future of absolute monarchs. And so unlike other leading aristocrats, such as his cousin Henry of Derby, Richard didn't joust—because of his poor health—although he liked hunting and hawking, as befitting a monarch of such radiance.

Art reflected this new order, and when Richard II ordered a royal portrait, the first king to have one drawn from life, he had himself painted with a gold crown, carrying a gold scepter and orb, and sitting on a chair in front of a gold wall. He also commissioned one of the finest surviving pieces of art of the time, the *Wilton Diptych*, which showed him besides Saint Edward, Saint Edmund, and Saint John, as well as the Virgin Mary; a fantastic piece of art, but perhaps one suggestive of a certain derangement. He left much to admire, rebuilding Westminster Hall and Westminster Abbey, and also had baths built at Sheen and Eltham palaces, which he visited due to his poor health.

The events of the 1380s were a repeat of the 1320s, and the same names even crop up again with different Warwicks and Lancasters. Richard at one point petitioned the pope to canonize Edward II on the grounds that he had died in defense of a holy cause—his right to be king—the implication being that anyone who tried to do the same to him would be damned.

Richard's enemies came to be known as the 'Lords Appellant,' and the cause of conflict, as with that previous reign, was the power and prestige he bestowed on his favorites, as well as lack of trustworthiness. The king was half-insane but his enemies were hardly a sympathetic bunch. In 1388, they passed a draconian act against begging and vagrancy, while they also tried to restrict education for the children of serfs, in contrast to the king's 1391 Statute of Mortmain ordering that money appropriated from a monastery should be distributed to the poor.

Worst of all the king's opponents was his insufferable uncle, Thomas of Woodstock, also confusingly called Buckingham as well as Gloucester. Thomas was a big burly man who liked fighting, but was angry that as the youngest son of Edward III he missed out on the chance to win glory in a French war, and was frustrated by his lack of opportunities for military triumphs. He was desperate for a fight and lamented that 'this is no life for men-at-arms who ought to win honor through deeds of arms and put their bodies to work.'

Woodstock had the famous family temper, but he was also affable and popular, with no sly side; he was not filled with the personal insecurity that drove his nephew. He was, however, very indiscreet, and said of the king that 'his backside has grown too fat, he's only interested in eating and drinking' and went further by adding: 'There's going to be serious trouble all over the country.'

Early in his reign, Richard had shocked the leading magnates by breaking his grandfather's will, a sign of things to come. The old king had left land for three monasteries so that monks could pray for his soul, but Richard tried to hand it over to Burley. The barons objected. His choice of bride in 1381 also disappointed many; the leading men wanted Richard to marry a daughter of the Duke of Milan—who had something like two dozen children—because she came with an enormous dowry, and the country was broke. Instead, he chose Anne, the sister of the Holy Roman emperor, paying her brother Wenzel the Drunkard twenty-thousand florins for the honor; later Richard entertained dreams of becoming the emperor himself, one of numerous deluded fantasies he entertained.[3]

The king needed money, and opportunity soon arose; at the end of 1381 the heir to the throne, Edmund Mortimer, the Earl of March, died during a scuffle with rebel chiefs in Ireland. He was just twenty-nine, joining a succession of luckless Mortimer men into an early grave; his father Roger had died at thirty-one and his grandfather Edmund at twenty-nine, while his great-grandfather Roger had made it to forty-three before being hanged by Edward III.

Richard had tried to get his hands on Mortimer's money, which should have gone to his widow and young children, but he was opposed by Woodstock and Thomas de Beauchamp, the Earl of Warwick, whose mother was a Mortimer. When Parliament met at Salisbury in November 1384, another of the king's critics, Richard Fitzalan, the Earl of Arundel, attacked the state of the government and the royal cronies. Arundel was the grandson of Henry of Lancaster and, along with Woodstock, was one of the main warmongers. The king listened and, after a pause, exploded in a rage shouting back that Arundel was a liar, and damning his soul to hell. There was stunned silence in the hall.

The bishops tried to step in as peacemakers, but when they organized a get-together it turned into a hysterical argument after a rumor spread that there was a plot against the king led by Gaunt.

Richard ordered the execution of the friar who started it, but a horrified Gaunt intervened, and so instead the man was led off to a nearby jail where he was tortured to death anyway by Burley, John Holland, and his gang. Even the jail keeper, who presumably had fairly low standards regarding human rights, was shocked by their excesses.

It later turned out that Richard had ordered Gaunt's execution, too, but his cronies had refused to carry it out. The king could not abide his uncle, and he increasingly felt threatened by him, although this paranoia was not entirely without merits. Gaunt is said to have forged a chronicle and had it placed in several monasteries, in which it was claimed his wife's great-grandfather, Edmund, first Earl of Lancaster, was actually Henry III's elder son rather than his brother Edward I, but had been set aside because of a deformity. This torturous theory would, of course, make his son Henry Bolingbroke the rightful king. Gaunt soon fled north after an attempt by one of his nephew's allies, the Earl of Mowbray, to arrest him with a pliant judge and have him executed.

At the next council meeting, William Courtenay, the archbishop of Canterbury, chastised Richard, and the king screamed back at him and ordered the archbishop's lands confiscated; the chancellor, Michael de la Pole, was so stunned he refused to carry out theorder.

Now Richard declared his intention to invade Scotland and sent for his mother to organize a meeting with Gaunt. The crown's policy toward Scotland had traditionally been to respond to raids by heading north, burning down Edinburgh, and then returning home and declaring victory; while the Scottish aristocracy would simply head beyond the River Forth, which was basically impossible to subjugate and besides which, there wasn't anything to conquer but wasteland. Gaunt urged his nephew to go further, but Richard refused his advice, and implied his uncle wanted him up in the wilds of Scotland so he could murder him. Which may well have crossed his mind.

Richard further entrenched his cronies; in November 1385, he made Parliament promote the lowborn de la Pole to Earl of Suffolk, and the following year he raised him to Duke of Ireland without even asking.

The king now had the chance to remove his main enemy. Gaunt had married Constance, daughter of the murdered Castilian king Pedro the Cruel, and had claimed the throne on behalf of his wife, even insisting on everyone calling him 'My Lord of Spain.' In 1385, Parliament had finally paid for Gaunt to go to Spain and claim the crown, and most people were happy to get rid of him, but without Gaunt the focus of opposition instead turned to Woodstock, who had all of his brother's belligerent instincts but none of his diplomatic skills.

Woodstock and his nephew were opposites in character and argued ferociously. Gaunt, as well as his brother Edmund, Duke of York, had tried to mediate and told Richard to be patient with Thomas, but with the elder brother away and York largely absent from politics, that restraint was gone too.

In 1386, Richard sent Michael de la Pole to demand of Parliament a fourfold increase in revenue; they responded by demanding de la Pole's impeachment. A no, in other words. The king said he would not dismiss a scullery maid for them, and withdrew, and the parliamentarians had to stay a month in London lodgings waiting for him to change his mind. The 1386 session that tried to audit the king came to be called the 'Wonderful Parliament.'

The monarch then announced, to his opponents' astonishment, that he would ask the French to help him with his financial troubles. Arundel and Woodstock warned him: 'Your people have an ancient law which, unfortunately, had to be invoked not so long ago,' a reference to his great-grandfather Edward II. Should a king 'rashly do just what he wants, then, with the people of the realm's assent and approval it is lawful to pull him down off his throne and put some near kinsmen in his place'—by which Woodstock presumably meant himself.

Richard went back to Parliament and sat through proceedings as de la Pole was impeached and thrown in jail. Within weeks the king simply ignored them by having him freed. At this point, to emphasize in people's minds how degenerate Richard's court was, De Vere left his wife, the king's own cousin, for one of the queen's ladies-in-waiting, Agnes de Launcekrona. Even De Vere's mother expressed shock at such scandalous behavior, but despite this indignity committed against his own relative, Richard soon afterwards gave De Vere a cushy job in Cheshire, far away from London.

From a twenty-first-century point of view, Richard's aversion to war seems not just moral but also sensible, but at the time it was believed, with good reason, that a country not led by a monarch in overseas conflict was likely to turn on itself. The war party had a lot of popular support, especially after March 1387 when Arundel led a fleet to attack a Flemish wine convoy sailing from La Rochelle to Sluys. He captured fifty Flemish ships with nineteen tuns of very good quality wine (a tun being 240 gallons), which was sold in London at a heavily reduced price. 'The praise of the Earl grew immensely among the commons,' it was recorded, as you'd imagine of anyone who came back with twenty-five thousand bottles of booze.

The king now made Lord and Commons swear that all acts restraining royal power were illegal, which was against Magna Carta. Richard also forced a group of magistrates and justices to agree to the arrest of dozens of parliamentarians who he viewed as 'traitors.' One of them, Justice Bealknap, objected to this blatantly illegal act and was punched in the face by De Vere, which was certainly against Magna Carta. Around this time, Richard showed further signs of megalomania, having 'discovered' a special oil supposedly given by the Virgin Mary to Thomas Becket, the twelfth-century archbishop of Canterbury who was hacked to death by the king's cronies.

The situation deteriorated so much that in November 1387 while the king was in London, Woodstock, Arundel, and Warwick swore an oath to one another, so becoming known as the Lords Appellants. Richard tried to raise an army in London but was met with apathy, and when confronted by the three men, he agreed to everything they demanded—then went back on his word.

Instead, he sent de la Pole to France to seek help from the king—who as it turns out was also showing the first signs of insanity—along with a basket of chickens to sell en route. The hapless de la Pole arrived first in Calais, but was recognized by local people; in a panic he went to his brother Edmund, the governor of a castle in the city, asking for his help. However, only weeks earlier one of Richard's knights had been caught carrying a message offering to hand Calais over to the French, and it was assumed de la Pole was doing the same. De la Pole's own brother now handed him over to the governor of Calais, who happened to be Warwick's brother William de Beauchamp, who was married to another of Arundel's daughters. De le Pole was arrested and sent back to King Richard, who didn't blame him for his failure but simply allowed him to go to Hull and escape the country again. He managed to leave this time.

De Vere had meanwhile raised five thousand men in Cheshire, the county where the monarch recruited men for battle with the Welsh and later the French. They were led by the constable of Cheshire Castle, Sir Thomas Molyneux, a ruthless and capable soldier who had men of his garrison who refused the call put in chains until his return. But Cheshire also bordered the lands of Lancaster, which was under the control of the king's cousin. Up and down the kingdom villages were emptying of men as the main lords prepared for battle; the country was heading for war.

CHAPTER TWELVE

Sad Stories
of the Death of Kings

M ad as the king was, he did at least promote art, and his supposedly effeminate court helped to spread the Italian culture into England at an exciting time. Back in 1373, the great humanist Giovanni Boccaccio had given a lecture in Florence on Dante, the Florentine poet whose *Divine Comedy,* written between 1308–1320, is widely considered one of the great masterpieces of all time. Among those in the city was an English spy called Geoffrey Chaucer who, in his capacity as a royal agent, had visited Italy several times. Chaucer came back changed by Italian poetry, and after further travel as a diplomat and pilgrim set about rewriting continental works in a new language of literature—English.

Ever since the Battle of Hastings, English had been a despised peasant tongue, while French was the language of law and court life in England, but in the fourteenth century it reemerged with a number of poets, among them John Gower, William Langland, and the unknown author of *Pearl.*[1] England and Normandy had been separated in 1204, by which stage most Anglo-Norman aristocrats were bilingual, but the court of Richard II was the first since 1066 to have English as its primary language.

However, the language had changed hugely; what was spoken in 1066 is called Old English and was very much like German. The *Anglo-Saxon Chronicle*, records kept by monks since the ninth century at five locations across the country, show the evolution of the language, so that the second-to-last entry, from 1135, is recognizably Old English; the last, made almost twenty years later, is noticeably different and what is now called Middle English.[2] The Norman conquest led to many French words entering English, although by far the largest influx came in the thirteenth and fourteenth centuries when French was the international language, and the University of Paris the very heart of western civilization.

Middle English is just about readable to us, although it contains much that looks like gobbledygook; Anglo-Saxon is utterly incomprehensible. Writing in the fifteenth century, William Caxton said of a piece of Old English that 'certaynly it was wreton in suchewyse that it was more lyke to Dutche than Englysshe: I coude not reduce ne brynge it to be understonden.'

The nationalistic war unleashed by Edward III may have heralded the final triumph of English, after which anyone seen as being too French was regarded as untrustworthy. In 1356, the same year as the battle in Poitiers, the mayor of London began proceedings in English, and Parliament followed in 1363. Around the same time, the king ordered that English must be spoken in law courts; legal documents were still written in French, but linguistic experts can work out from the syntax that they were originally thought out in English. One bizarre theory about the Plague is that it might especially have hit French speakers, concentrated more in dangerous professions like the clergy, and so there was no one left to teach what was still then the language of official business. Certainly knowledge of the language must have become uncommon, for a surviving will from 1400 by James de Peckham bequeaths 'all my books in French to those who know how to use them.'

Among the early writers of the new language, the London

vintner's son Geoffrey Chaucer was the greatest. Chaucer started off penning romantic poetry, or what he described as 'the craft of fyn lovynge,' but his most famous work, *The Canterbury Tales*, is a very bawdy account of a group of travelers on pilgrimage to Rome. These religious tours were the cheap package holidays of the day, which is why Lollards didn't approve, and the dialogue—filled with references to 'turds' and the like—reflects this. 'The Knight's Tale' is full of sex and lurid stories, among the lines: 'Derk was the nyght as pich, or as the cole, And at the wyndow out she putte hir hole.'

As well as being an author, Chaucer did some work for the crown, almost certainly as a spy, and would regularly go abroad on 'the King's secret business,' and he was also ambassador to the powerful Italian city-state of Genoa. The trip there was not fun: his contemporary Adam of Usk described going across the Alps 'drawn in an ox-wagon half dead with cold, and my eyes blindfolded lest I should see the dangers of the pass.' And that was a picnic compared to the journey across the English Channel.

Chaucer was recruiting mercenaries against the French in Genoa, as well as acting as a trade ambassador, but while there, he was heavily influenced by the cultural flowering and, in Italy, may even have met Boccaccio and Petrarch, the great poets of the day. Among the other things he brought back from Italy, Chaucer perhaps brought the idea of celebrating 'Seynt Valentynes day' to England, which previously had no romantic connection.

The poet was supported by John of Gaunt, who was his brother-in-law as the two men were married to sisters, and for his work Edward III awarded Chaucer 'a gallon of wine daily for the rest of his life,' which is normally a good way of putting a writer out of business. Annoyingly, however, it was only for the rest of Edward's life, and he died three years later.

Chaucer also had spells as an MP, a forester, a foreman for royal building projects, a justice of the peace in Kent, and an excise man, and at one point he collected a quarter of the crown's revenue through customs, getting the cushy job of 'controller of the petty custom.' The poet was also given the task of carrying large amounts of money for the crown, a dangerous role, and he was robbed twice, first in Deptford and then Westminster—a little over nine pounds stolen the second time around. The villains were caught and one turned evidence so they did trial by battle, as was the custom; the loser was hanged.

In 1387, Richard II also granted Chaucer a large cask of wine each year, but it failed to arrive. He was still doing the 'king's arduous and urgent business' years later, and was given a scarlet gown lined with fur by the king in 1400, but after that year no more is heard of him. His tomb, erected a century later, lists his death as October 25, 1400, and one theory is that he was murdered, which would not have been surprising considering the homicide rate at the time. Chaucer was the first poet buried in Westminster Abbey, but not because of his great work, but in recognition for his work as a customs official; two hundred years later another poet, Edmund Spenser, was laid there, and so that part of the building became known as Poets' Corner; the most recent burial there was of actor Sir Laurence Olivier, in 1988.

The year Chaucer died was also bad for Richard II, a sad time in his life chronicled by a far more famous English writer.

The End

The three Appellants now became five, joined by Thomas Mowbray, who was Arundel's son-in-law, and Gaunt's heir Henry Bolingbroke. No one actually called him Bolingbroke at the time, rather he was known as the Earl of Derby, but largely thanks to William Shakespeare it's just easier to call him that. Richard and Henry were the same age, had spent much of their childhood together, and were even in the Tower of London together for much of the terrifying summer of 1381, but they were totally unalike.

Bolingbroke had grown up in Hertford Castle in 'the rough and tumble of chivalry,'[3] and in 1376, then aged nine, he had been sent by his father to live with his cousin. The two did not get on. Henry was already at this age obsessed with sports and wished to become the finest jouster in Europe; Richard was more interested in reading Giles of Rome explain why God had chosen him to have absolute power over everyone. As far as he was concerned, Henry's world of chivalry and aristocratic violence was the past, while lawyers and courtiers were the future.

As a young man, Henry went on Crusade against the heathens of Lithuania, the last remaining corner of Europe that was pagan. He made sure regular dispatches of newsletters about his doings were sent back so everyone heard about them; whether or not he had ambitions, he was trying to build an image of himself as a heroic figure.

A year before almost dying at the hands of the mob, Bolingbroke had become very wealthy through his marriage to twelve-year-old Mary de Bohun, younger daughter of the fantastically rich Earl of Hereford. His uncle Woodstock had already married her elder sister and tried to force Mary into a nunnery in order to grab all the inheritance for himself, but while away in France, Gaunt had his son wed to her. This fired up their rivalry. Meanwhile, the county palatinate of Lancaster would pass to Bolingbroke through his mother Blanche, making him even wealthier.

The five Appellants had raised armies, and on December 19, 1387, they beat a force led by De Vere consisting of five thousand Cheshire archers at the Battle of Radcot Bridge. Although Thomas Molyneux had a dagger stuck into his eye, De Vere had made a remarkable escape through the mist and rode back on his horse along the Thames toward London, bringing the disastrous news to his king.

In the 'Merciless' Parliament that started in February, the Appellants had four of the king's cronies, confusingly called the

'Appellees,' impeached and executed; yet the Appellants were dis-united about how to proceed. Woodstock wanted the throne himself, and while Arundel supported him, Mowbray and Bolingbroke, his senior in succession terms, opposed the idea. There were too many divisions within the rebel ranks, and Richard survived. De Vere, de la Pole, and two others who had left the country were convicted of treason in his absence and sentenced to death. Of all of the king's favorites, only Sir Nicholas Brembre, a former lord mayor of Lon-don, refused to flee. He threw down his gloves and offered to fight anyone who would take him up; three hundred gloves came down in response, which was probably not the response he was hoping for. He was later hanged. Another favorite, the Cornish lawyer Robert Tresilian, was found hiding in the Sanctuary of Westminster and executed on the spot.

Even Simon Burley got it, although Mowbray and Bolingbroke both saw him as a father figure and tried to save his life, but were voted down. After three months of the Merciless Parliament, all of Richard's friends had been dragged to their deaths or exiled. De la Pole died in Paris in 1389; another favorite, Alexander Neville, expired in Louvain in the Low Countries in 1392. Robert De Vere had made it to Flanders where, in 1392, he was killed by a wild boar.

The year following the purge, in May 1389, Richard took full control as an adult. He proclaimed: 'We have reached the age of majority, already in our twenty-second year.' The king told his lords that his wife had convinced him to forgive his enemies; all were sat-isfied that the past could be put behind them.

In fact, the king was intent on revenge and had gathered around him a group of followers, an 'affinity,' who adopted Richard's sym-bol of the white hart as a mark of membership, such badges having come into fashion among aristocratic factions. They would continue to be used in the next century of fighting and survive today in many English village pubs; Richard II also introduced legislation forcing taverns and inns to adopt names, which is why the White Hart is the fifth most popular pub name today.

Richard continued to hate his uncle Woodstock, who was told to go to Ireland but refused. Woodstock said the Irish were 'a nasty, beggarly people with a perfectly beastly country which is quite uninhabitable—even if we conquered all of it within a year, they'd take the whole lot back from us inside another.'

The king's behavior could be strange. In 1392, after falling out with the people of London, Richard demanded a great pageantry of coronation proportions in the capital as an apology; he and his queen, Anne of Bohemia, proceeded through the city in splendor, with boys dressed as angels behind them. The royal couple continued to demand and receive gifts from their subjects; in January 1393, Richard was sent a camel, and Anne a pelican.

The king could be unpredictably violent, but after his wife's death in 1394, his behavior became increasingly erratic. Arundel arrived late at Westminster Abbey for Anne's requiem, and begged to be excused, but the king seized a cane and hit him over the head, the earl falling with blood running down the pavement. Richard would have killed him were he not in church, and Arundel spent several weeks in the Tower and was fined a vast amount. Richard had Sheen Palace, where his wife had died, razed to the ground; ever obsessed with ceremony, he delayed his wife's funeral for two months so the right sort of wax torches could be brought from Flanders.

The leading figures in the realm were keen for the childless thirty-two-year-old to remarry but were less than impressed with his choice of bride, who was just seven; they might not expect an adult heir for thirty years, by which time the mentally unstable king might be dead, or worse, still alive. Richard's new bride Isabel was the daughter of Charles VI of France, who was younger than his new son-in-law, and she came with a dowry of nearly £170,000, which was much needed, but the war party feared it meant the end of their dreams of further rampages across France.

Richard, meanwhile, seemed to be losing his mind, his actions suggesting 'a sudden loss of control, the onset of a mental malaise,' in the words of a leading historian: 'If Richard was sane from 1397 onwards, it was with the sanity of a man who pulls his own house down about his ears.'[4] For while all along the king had pretended to forgive his enemies, he was waiting for his revenge, and in July that year Arundel was invited to a dinner with the king, and, unaware of what was happening, was arrested and sentenced to death. In September, he sent armed retainers to Woodstock's home Pleshey Castle in Essex, waking him and having him arrested too. 'You will have the same mercy you showed to Sir Simon Burley,' Richard told his uncle.

Woodstock was taken to Calais where 'just before dinner, when the tables were laid in the castle and the duke was on the point of washing his hands, four men came out of the next room and putting a towel round his neck they strangled him, two of them pulling at each head.'[5] Then they undressed the body and put it in the bed and went back and told everyone he'd had an apoplectic fit.

The king now called Parliament, filling it with his own supporters to ensure the Appellants would go through the same ordeal he had. The king forbade anyone to bring arms, on pain of death, and had Parliament ringed with three hundred loyal archers from Cheshire, who affectionately called him 'Dykon.' Some of the soldiers bent their arrows back to their ears at one point, terrifying the crowded chamber; in this tense, nervous atmosphere a trigger-happy archer accidentally fired into the crowd, although no one was hurt.

Gaunt was forced into taking part in this show trial: Arundel was sentenced to death, while Warwick escaped execution after groveling, and was instead sent to the Isle of Man to live in poverty. When the time came for Gaunt to pass sentence on his brother, it was learned that Woodstock was already dead. The children of Arundel, Warwick, and Woodstock were also disinherited, and their land distributed to Richard's supporters. The king said everyone would be pardoned except fifty 'unknown individuals' whom he did not name, which did not exactly make everyone feel comfortable.

Then, in July 1398, Roger Mortimer, fourth Earl of March and heir to the throne, was killed in Ireland in a fight, aged just twenty-four, which he must have been half expecting considering his family history. Richard made plans to go to Ireland to seek justice.

At this point, the two remaining Appellants fell out. Following the execution of his father-in-law, Mowbray had approached Bolingbroke with a plan to unseat the king; Bolingbroke, unnerved, had told his father who then informed Richard. The two men then accused each other of lying. Richard decreed that as gentlemen they should have a fight, which was arranged for September 1398. People came from all over Europe for this enormous event, the ultimate way to solve a celebrity feud. But just as they were about to get down to it, the king stopped proceedings and ordered both men banished from the kingdom, Mowbray for life and Bolingbroke for ten years, with the condition he could return when his father died. Mowbray left for Venice, where he fell victim to the Plague the following year.

In 1399, John of Gaunt also passed away, but Richard, now 'a mumbling neurotic sinking rapidly into a state of complete melancholia,' had all his son's lands confiscated.[6] The king then embarked for Ireland to meet with local chiefs and Anglo-Irish lords, a quite successful mission as it turned out.[7] However, while he was there, Bolingbroke landed in Yorkshire to reclaim his property; marching south, Henry amassed followers and it must have occurred to him at some point that he must either take the crown or nothing (maybe he thought this before launching the invasion).

Richard was isolated, and when he landed in Wales on July 24, he found that everyone had turned to his rival. Even the Cheshire archers had deserted him, while Henry's supporters captured Chester, his greatest stronghold. Richard fled to Conwy Castle, sending John Montacute—the Earl of Salisbury, and one of the last men loyal to him—to raise a Welsh army. Montacute as a young man

had fought against the pagan Slavs in Prussia alongside Bolingbroke, and the latter's eldest son Henry was entrusted to him after
the boy's mother had died; but despite this, he stood by the king
even as his support faded. However, when Richard arrived at the
castle he found that Montacute had just one hundred men, which
must have been dispiriting to say the least.

Now the king's uncle Edmund came over to Bolingbroke, who
began executing regime men, among them the Earl of Wiltshire,
Richard's treasurer, as well as two members of the royal council,
Sir John Bussy and Sir Henry Green, considered 'chief aiders and
abettors of his malevolence.'⁸ Richard might have fled to France or
Ireland, but now deluded, he thought he would defeat his enemies
and 'one day . . . skin them alive.' The Earl of Northumberland
lured him out of the castle, swearing on the Communion Host that
he could keep his throne if only he restored the Duchy of Lancaster
to Henry; instead, Richard was seized and taken to Chester. When
his greyhound licked the face of Bolingbroke when they met, the
king muttered to himself that this was a bad omen. On the way
down to London, Richard had tried to escape out a window of the
carriage, to no avail.

Having been captured, he refused to give up his crown in favor
of his cousin, and instead put his ceremonial circlet on the ground,
symbolically abdicating to God, which probably made him feel
better, although the end result was still the same. On October 21,
1399, Richard was brought along the Thames, 'weeping and loudly
bewailing he had ever been born.'⁹ There, a knight told him: 'You
may remember how you treated the Earl of Arundel in just the same
way, always with the utmost cruelty.'

In the capital, the fallen king was greeted with jeers and pelted
with rubbish from the rooftops, the mob always ready to turn on
anyone who was obviously a loser, and at his own request he was
placed in the Tower of London. A list of charges was read out and,
terrified of what awaited him, the king cowardly blamed four of his

household knights for the deaths of Arundel and Woodstock. These four men were now summoned and taken to a room next door to the king where they were tied to a horse's tail, dragged through the city, and had their heads cut off with a fishmonger's knife.

The chronicler Froissart recorded that 'King Richard was in terrible anguish, knowing he was trapped and in danger from the Londoners. He thought every man in England was against him . . . he began to cry.' Adam of Usk, one of Bolingbroke's confederates, went to the king to persuade him to give up his throne; drunk, the monarch groaned, 'My God, this is a false, treacherous country, toppling, destroying and killing so many kings, rulers, great men. It never stops being torn apart by quarrels, strife, and hatred.'

Usk remembered how he used to be a once radiant monarch, and 'I took my leave deeply moved, recalling his former splendor.' No more is heard from Richard. His supporters, led by Montacute, hatched a plot to free him over the feast of the Epiphany, January 6, 1400, and to have him placed on the throne again, after killing Henry at a tournament. It was foiled, and while the old king's fate remains unclear—officially Richard died while on a hunger strike a few months later—one doesn't have to be a deluded conspiracy theorist to suspect it was murder. Montacute was meanwhile executed, as were all those implicated in the plot, all except one man whom Bolingbroke pardoned—an old soldier named John Ferrour.

The new king, Henry IV, the first to speak English as a mother tongue since 1066, opened his first Parliament by shouting along with the barons 'Yes! Yes! Yes!' when asked whether he wanted to be king before asking them to shout it again with him, louder this time. For his coronation, he had himself anointed with the special oil given to Thomas Beckett by the Virgin Mary herself, the stuff that Richard II had supposedly found. But during the service, lice emerged from his hair, and a further omen of doom came when he dropped the ceremonial gold coin given to him by the archbishop. It rolled away, never to be found, a sign from God—Henry was a usurper and a usurper he would remain. Bolingbroke's life would soon fall apart, his health would rapidly decline, and after more than a decade of struggle with rebellious lords he would be convinced he was cursed by God.

To overthrow a monarch was a great and heinous act, and one that men dreaded to act upon for fear of what it might bring. And with good reason, for this was the prelude to decades of conflict in which Edward III's descendants tore one another to pieces; by the time the war between the Houses of Lancaster and York was finished, three more kings had suffered violent deaths and countless noblemen were dead with them. The War of the Roses had begun.

Bibliography

This book is a short and simplified account of the period, which is well covered by historians in books and publications—at both academic and popular level—a very, very small sample of which can be found below.

Ackroyd, Peter. *Chaucer*
Ackroyd, Peter. *Foundations*
Ashley, Mike. *British Kings and Queens*
Audley, Anselm. *Death Keeps His Court*
Barker, Juliet. *England Arise*
Carpenter, David. *Magna Carta*
Castor, Helen. *She-Wolves*
Clark, Stephen. *1000 Years of Annoying the French*
Fraser, Antonia. *The Lives of the Kings and Queens of England*
Gillingham, John. *Conquests, Catastrophe and Recovery*
Gimson, Andrew. *Gimson's Kings and Queens*
Harvey, John. *The Plantagenets*
Hibbert, Christopher. *The English: A Social History*
Holmes, George. *The Later Middle Ages 1272–1485*
Jenkins, Simon. *A Short History of England*
Jones, Dan. *Plantagenets*

Jones, Dan. *Realm Divided*

Jones, Dan. *Summer of Blood*

Jones, Terry. *Medieval Lives*

Kelly, John. *The Great Mortality*

Lacey, Robert. *Great Tales from English History*

Manchester, William. *A World Lit Only By Fire*

McKisack, May. *The Fourteenth Century*

Morris, Marc. *A Great and Terrible King*

Mortimer, Ian. *A Time Traveller's Guide to Medieval England*

Mortimer, Ian. *The Perfect King*

Myers, A. R. *England in the Late Middle Ages*

Ormrod, W. H. *The Kings and Queens of England*

Palmer, Alan. *Kings and Queens of England*

Rose, Alexander. *Kings in the North*

Saul, Nigel. *For Honour and Fame*

Schama, Simon. *A History of Britain*

Seward, Desmond. *A Brief History of the 100 Years War*

Seward, Desmond. *The Demon's Brood*

Speck, W. A. *A Concise History of Britain*

Strong, Roy. *A History of Britain*

Sumption, Jonathan. *Edward III*

Tombs, Robert. *The English and Their History*

Tuchman, Barbara. *A Distant Mirror*

West, Richard. *Chaucer*

White, R. J. *A Short History of England*

Whittock, Martyn. *A Brief History of Life in the Middle Ages*

Wilson, Derek. *The Plantagenets*

Winder, Robert. *Bloody Foreigners*

Ziegler, Philip. *The Black Death*

Endnotes

Introduction

1. Old St Paul's, as it's known to historians, was only finally completed that year, having been started in 1087. It burned down in 1666 during the Great Fire of London.
2. St Paul's Annalist.
3. Although estimating historical populations is mostly guesswork, the population of England certainly fell by about half, which clearly suggests it wasn't a great time to be alive. During the famine, it fell by between 5–15 percent from 1315 to 1325, and declined by 30–40 percent during the Plague year of 1348–49, and a further 15–25 percent in rest of the century after repeat attacks of the disease.
4. Wharram Percy in Yorkshire.

Chapter One

1. Because there were three Edwards in a row, people began to distinguish them as I, II, and III, even though before the Norman Conquest there had been kings now known as Edward the Elder, Edward the Martyr, and Edward the Confessor. It makes no sense, but it's too late to change it now.

2. Edward was responsible for the two Statutes of Westminster, in 1275 and 1290, and the Statute of Winchester, which established firmly the status of Parliament.

3. See my amazing and brilliant book on this subject, *1215 and All That*.

4. Eleanor was descended from the Prophet Mohammed and since, according to one calculation, over 90 percent of English people are descended from their grandson Edward III, as well as a large percentage of western Europeans and North Americans, the chances are you, the reader, are, as well.

5. As a rule, all the worst and most evil or incompetent kings in English history—William the Conqueror, Edward, George III—were faithful and monogamous, and the most effective and humane were compulsive adulterers. Charles II was the first to show religious tolerance and pretty much every aristocrat in England traces their ancestry to one of his mistresses.

6. According to a common myth, when the fifteen-year-old Edward married the nine-year-old Eleanor of Castile, many inns were named after the Infanta (princess); one of which, located in a village south of London, became known to the largely illiterate population as the Elephant and Castle. But the story is probably untrue—records of the pub only date to the eighteenth century, when it was run by an Indian trading company that used as its logo an elephant with a large saddle, which could be mistaken for a castle.

7. Morris, Marc, *A Great and Terrible King.*

8. While on Crusade, Edward had run up debts of three thousand *livre tournois* to bankers in Acre and another seven thousand *pounds tournois* to Italian merchants. In a sign of things to come, he had to ask the pope to allow a special tax on clergy when he got back.

Chapter Two

1. The southern part of Pembrokeshire has been called Little England beyond Wales since at least the sixteenth century, while Flemish,

the language of what is now Belgium, was still spoken there as late as the 1580s.

2. The historian Paul Johnson suggests that the expulsion of the Jews cost England a huge amount.

Chapter Three

1. That's football. Or soccer, to you.
2. The film even includes the *Droite de Siegneur*, the idea that a nobleman could sleep with a peasant's wife on their wedding night, probably the most common untrue myth about the Middle Ages, along with belief in a flat earth and chastity belts. It never happened.
3. Tombs, Robert, *The English and Their History.*
4. However, it was all okay as she repented on her deathbed, for 'after she had devotedly received the sacrament of the dying, she earnestly prayed her lord the king . . . that everything unjustly taken from anyone by her or her ministers should be restored.'
5. The most famous is Charing Cross, by Trafalgar Square, although that is a replica.
6. Or it was the Earl of Surrey. We don't entirely know.
7. As for the film's suggestion that it was Wallace who got Queen Isabella pregnant, and who was therefore the real father of Edward III: Isabella was nine when Wallace died, and she hadn't even been to Britain yet.
8. Morris, Marc, *A Great and Terrible King.*
9. The story probably isn't true and only first appeared three centuries later and was about someone else.
10. Gillingham, John, *Conquests, Catastrophe and Recovery.*

Chapter Four

1. Gimson, Andrew, *Gimson's Kings and Queens.*
2. Carpenter, Christine, *War of the Roses.*
3. According to late Victorian historian Thomas Frederick Tout.
4. Castor, Helen, *She-Wolves.*
5. Seward, Desmond, *The Demon's Brood.*

6. He had a wide knowledge of literature, unusual among the higher nobility of his time, and we can see in him a foreshadowing of that strange marriage between culture and sadism that was to lend a special horror to some figures of the next century.

7. According to the *Vita Edwardi Secundi*, a chronicle written in 1326.

8. Gaveston is luckily immortalized in the name of a particularly decadent ball among Oxford undergraduates, where according to one book published in 2015, the future prime minister David Cameron is alleged to have had intimate relations with a dead pig. The whole thing was extremely unlikely, although Piers either way surely wouldn't have judged him.

9. It wasn't all plain sailing. While the royal couple were at Pontoise, a fire broke out in the English royal pavilion; many possessions were lost and Isabella's arms were burned.

10. Four centuries later, Norwegians returned to Greenland, one motive being to convert their long-lost cousins from Catholicism to Protestantism, but found no traces of them. The colony probably lasted until 1450, and was either massacred by Inuit or starved.

11. Ziegler, Philip, *The Black Death*.

12. The original, literal meaning of the word was to leave one's race, or *gen*.

13. Morris, Marc, *A Great and Terrible King*.

14. According to Gregory Clark of the University of California.

15. Tuchman, Barbara, *A Distant Mirror*.

16. Tuchman, Barbara, *A Distant Mirror*.

17. Castor, Helen, *She-Wolves*.

18. Harvey, John, *The Plantagenets*.

19. This story is treated with a great deal of scepticism by historians. Either way, he was murdered and it wasn't very nice.

Chapter Five

1. Some historians say Edward III was the first king to speak English since the Battle of Hastings, although some previous kings, such as Henry I, may have spoken it reasonably well.

2. Harvey, John, *The Plantagenets.*
3. Sumption, Jonathan, *Edward III.*
4. Sumption, Jonathan, *Edward III.*
5. Wilson, Derek, *The Plantagenets.*
6. Seward, Desmond, *The Demon's Brood.*
7. Tyburn became such a part of folklore that it spawned the phrase 'one for the road'—every condemned prisoner was allowed a pint of ale, one for the road, at a pub in Oxford Street. Apparently, almost every single prisoner made the same joke—'I'll settle my tab next time,' which the barman was presumably supposed to laugh at. Having said that, this theory is disputed.
8. Jenkins, Simon, *A Short History of England.*
9. The conflict is divided into the Edwardian War (1337–1360), the Caroline War (1369–1389), and Lancastrian War (1415–1455).
10. Guyenne, or Aquitaine, is the name for the larger region of southwest France of which Gascony was just one small part.
11. Seward, Desmond, *The Demon's Brood.*
12. Seward, Desmond, *The Demon's Brood.*
13. From Graham Robb's *The Discovery of France.* All in all there are fifty-five separate dialects in France, even today.
14. Even after the end of the Hundred Years' War, the region maintained strong ties with the English, held together by claret, rugby, and religion, being one of the most Protestant regions in later times.
15. Sumption, Jonathan, *Edward III.*
16. Froissart wrote: 'Any man who is King of that country must conform to the will of the people and bow to many of their wishes. If he fails to do this, and misfortune comes to the country, he will be thrown over.'
17. K. B. McFarlane, an early twentieth-century medieval historian.
18. This, however, is disputed, and some sources state his father was a wealthy landowner.
19. Sumption, Jonathan, *Edward III.*

20. The new coins from 1344, the gold nobles, half nobles, and quarter nobles, bore the words: *'Four things our noble showeth unto me, King, ship and sword, and power of the sea.'*
21. Sumption, Jonathan, *Edward III.*
22. Jones, Dan, *Summer of Blood.*
23. Recalled by contemporary Geoffrey le Baker.

Chapter Six

1. Seward, Desmond, *The Demon's Brood.*
2. He was not called the Black Prince until several centuries later.
3. Tuchman, Barbara, *A Distant Mirror.*
4. This was famously depicted in the popular 1799 painting by Benjamin West, *Queen Philippa Interceding for the Lives of the Burghers of Calais,* as well as the Rodin statue *The Burghers of Calais.*
5. Some spoilsports say this incident never actually happened. https://www.theguardian.com/education/2002/aug/15/highereducation.news.
6. Saul, Nigel, *For Honour and Fame.*
7. Tuchman, Barbara, *A Distant Mirror.*
8. https://en.wikipedia.org/wiki/Church_of_the_Annunciation _of_Our_Lady_of_the_Newarke.
9. Much of the story about George the Martyr had been mixed up with a Mediterranean fertility god, and the name comes from the Greek word for 'farmer.'

Chapter Seven

1. The poor Crimean Tartars were later the unlucky victims of Stalin's insane paranoia, and he had half the population deported to Uzbekistan. They were allowed back to Crimea in the 1980s and when Ukraine became independent in 1991, they were finally freed from Russian rule—until Russia invaded again.
2. Ziegler, Philip, *The Black Death.*
3. Ziegler, Philip, *The Black Death.*

4. Ziegler, Philip, *The Black Death.*
5. In 2013, workmen tunneling on the new Crossrail line in Charter-house Square, central London, uncovered a dozen skeletons from a fourteen-century plague pit.
6. Wilson, Derek, *The Plantagenets.*
7. According to contemporary chronicler Henry Knighton.
8. I. F. C. Hecker, *The Black Death in the Fourteenth Century.*
9. Other sources state that living sailors were aboard upon arrival.
10. Ziegler, Philip, *The Black Death.*
11. Land in the Rhine Valley in 1300 was worth seventeen times what it was in 900, which illustrates the economic growth at the time. In contrast, many areas have not recovered: Neufobourg in Normandy had a population of 3,000 in 1310 and 3,347 in 1954.
12. Some writers were skeptical of the University of Paris explana-tion, among them Konrade of Megenberg. One Muslim scholar, Ibn al Khatib, also disagreed with Islamic theology that denied the Plague could be spread by human-to-human infection, stating correctly that 'the existence of infection is firmly established by experience, research, mental perception, autopsy, and authentic knowledge of fact.'
13. Myers, A. R., *England in the Later Middle Ages.*
14. Ziegler, Philip, *The Black Death.*
15. Mortimer, Ian, *The Time Traveller's Guide to Medieval England.*
16. Tuchman, Barbara, *A Distant Mirror.*
17. There was a tiny remnant left similar to the remaining Jewish pop-ulations of Middle Eastern countries today, such as Afghanistan, where following the years of war and religious repression there were just two Jews left as of 2013. They weren't on speaking terms, after an ancient argument.
18. Jones, Terry, *Medieval Lives.*

Chapter Eight
1. Tuchman, Barbara, *A Distant Mirror.*
2. Tombs, Robert, *The English and Their History.*

3. The heirs to the French throne were called the dauphin because in 1349 the French had been allowed to annex the region of Dauphin. The dolphins on the royal coat of arms is a pun.

4. As a rough conversion, one pound at the time would be equivalent to one thousand dollars today, although true exchange rates are difficult as most basic products were so much more expensive.

5. Tuchman, Barbara, *A Distant Mirror.*

6. Sumption, Jonathan, *Edward III.*

7. Seward, Desmond, *The Demon's Brood.*

8. McKisack, May, *The Fourteenth Century.*

9. Fourteenth-century poet John Gower.

Chapter Nine

1. No one used the word 'peasants' at the time and some historians argue that the term is inappropriate for England's social structure, in which there was a market in land already, but it stuck.

2. Carpenter, David, *Magna Carta.*

3. To be fair, Froissart said of the English as a whole that they were 'men of a haughty disposition, hot tempered and quickly moved to anger, difficult to pacify and to bring to sweet reason. They take delight in battles and slaughter. They are extremely covetous of the possessions of others, and are incapable by nature of joining in friendship or alliance with a foreign nation.' And he added 'there are no more untrustworthy people under the sun than the middle classes in England.'

4. Public schools, which in the United States would be called private schools, were open to people who weren't in holy orders (i.e., the public). Just to make things more confusing, the British also say 'private schools' but not all private schools are public schools. If you can understand that then the rules of cricket shouldn't be too difficult.

5. Barker, Juliet, *England Arise.*

6. France also tried to restrict wages, allowing a price rise of up to a third of the previous level, which was somewhat more realistic.

7. Tuchman, Barbara, *A Distant Mirror.*

8. Tyler might have been from Colchester in Essex originally.

9. Hales, Bishop Courtenay, Bishop Fordum, Chief Justice Sir Robert Belknap, Sir Ralph Ferrers, Sir Robert Plessington, Chief Baron of the Exchequer, John Legge, John de Brampton.

10. Two centuries later, these parts of England would become the home of the argumentative and fanatical Puritan sect that later went to New England to create their crazed utopia. This 'United States of America' they then founded soon fell into obscurity.

11. Both Cambridge and Oxford were subject to numerous riots in this period between townsmen and scholars, the most recent being Oxford's St. Scholastica Day riot of 1354, which left more than sixty students and thirty locals dead.

12. They were also influenced by Edward I's 1285 Statute of Winchester.

13. Jones, Dan, *Realm Divided.*

14. Or possibly Maidstone.

15. There is debate about the circumstances of Tyler's death, and who drew a weapon first and why. Suffice it to say that the meeting didn't go well for him.

16. Tombs, Robert, *The English and Their History.*

17. This is a British in-joke. The Conservative government introduced a poll tax in 1989 that led to rioting and the downfall of Prime Minister Margaret Thatcher, whose replacement immediately abolished it again. Someone will probably try again in two hundred years, just because.

18. Whittock, Martyn, *A Brief History of Life in the Middle Ages.*

19. Myers, A. R., *England in the Late Middle Ages.*

Chapter Ten

1. The death rates from Plague were higher among the clergy, and in York and Lincoln the death rate was 40 percent, but as high as 50 percent in Herefordshire and the Southwest.

2. According to medieval historian Barbara Harvey.

3. Ackroyd, Peter, *Chaucer*.

4. Hawkwood had become so powerful in Italy as to be something of a statesman, and when he died in 1395, the city promised him a marble tomb in the Duomo, although they instead sent his body back to England after the English offered to pay them. It's not like they actually liked him.

5. Jones, Terry, *Medieval Lives*.

6. Thomas of Walsingham's verdict on the expedition.

Chapter Eleven

1. Seward, Desmond, *The Demon's Brood*.

2. Harriss, G. L., *Shaping the Nation*.

3. Wenzel was notorious for a number of incidences, some of which might be true, but he certainly threw the vicar-general John of Pomuk off a bridge after prolonged torture. As a result, John became the patron saint of bridges, a niche market.

Chapter Twelve

1. *Pearl* is a deeply moving poem written by an unknown author from Cheshire or Lancashire, judging by the dialect. The Pearl in question is his departed daughter.

2. The last text described as Old English dates from the 1190s, seventy years after the first Middle English text, so change was slow and uneven.

3. Audley, Anselm, *Death Keeps His Court*.

4. McKisack, May, *The Fourteenth Century*.

5. Wilson, Derek, *The Plantagenets*.

6. Seward, Desmond, *The Demon's Brood*.

7. Richard was popular in Ireland and visited there once before, where he was, unusually for English monarchs, quite just.

8. *Chronicle of Adam of Usk*, a Welsh priest of the period.

9. *Chronicle of Adam of Usk*.